Stuff That SCARES Your Pants Off!

The SCIENCE SCOOP on more than 30 TERRIFYING PHENOMENA!

by Glenn Murphy

Rb
Flash
Point

ROARING BROOK PRESS
NEW YORK

To Damon, Debs, and Gaby—for being fearless

in the face of risky book ideas

Text copyright © 2011 by Glenn Murphy
Illustrations copyright © 2011 by Mike Phillips

Published by Flash Point, an imprint of Roaring Brook Press
Roaring Brook Press is a division of Holtzbrinck Publishing Holdings Limited Partnership
175 Fifth Avenue, New York, New York 10010
www.mackids.com

Library of Conress Cataloging-in-Publication Data

Murphy, Glenn.
    Stuff that scares your pants off! : a book of scary things (and how to avoid them) / Glenn Murphy ;
illustrated by Mike Phillips. — 1st American ed.
        p. cm.
    Includes bibliographical references and index.
    ISBN 978-1-59643-633-6 (alk. paper)
    1. Fear—Juvenile literature. 2. Social psychology—Juvenile literature.
I. Phillips, Mike, 1961– ill. II. Title.
BF575.F2M935 2011
001.9—dc22

                                                    2010027541

Roaring Brook Press books are available for special promotions and premiums.
For details contact: Director of Special Markets, Holtzbrinck Publishers.
First Published in the United Kingdom by Macmillan Children's Books.
First American Edition September 2010

Book design by Andrew Arnold

Printed in July 2011 in the United States of America by RR Donnelley & Sons Company, Willard, Ohio

10 9 8 7 6 5 4 3 2 1

Thanks to:
    Damon McCollin-Moore, Deborah Bloxam, Fran Bate, Sarah Richardson, Katie Maggs, Rob Skitmore and everyone at the
Science Museum who offered their ideas and comments.
    Gaby Morgan and everyone at Macmillan Children's Books, for continuing transatlantic support.
    Dr. Annabel Price.
    Julia Hewlett and Professor Alun Williams from the Royal Veterinary College.
    Jane, Omar, Brad, and Victoria—for putting me up (and putting up with me) during the summer book tour in London—the
Mitcham Massive lives on.
    The Schwichows, the Sherrills, the Fab Four (well, the other three), and all our new friends in NC.
    The Witts and the Murphys.
    And, as always, Heather and the Fuzzball—couldn't do this without you.

CONTENTS

INTRODUCTION

Shark attacks. Plane crashes. Deadly diseases. Ghosts, monsters, and aliens. This book is jam-packed with bad, scary stuff, and covers just about anything that you could possibly be afraid of.

But this is more than a big book of "bad" and "scary." It's a journey into fear itself.

Along the way, we'll travel deep into the unknown territories of the mind and body, searching for the roots and workings of fear, phobias, and panic.

We'll look at what fears are, where they come from, and how to work with them, live with them, and get around them. We'll explore the wide world of things that make people afraid, and weigh up how scary they really are. We'll look at the chances of the bad stuff really happening, and we'll give you the lowdown on how to avoid it.

From earthquakes and hurricanes to spiders and snakes; from doctors and dentists to planes, trains, and car crashes; from darkness and drowning to ghosts and the Great Beyond—we'll face every terror in our quest for understanding. With a bit of biology, a spot of psychology, and oodles of lovely facts and figures, we'll learn everything there is to know about our fears. We'll see how they begin, how they build and balloon into phobias, and how we can use our new knowledge to stop fear and panic in their tracks.

Sound good to you? Or scary, perhaps?
How about both?

Good and scary—that's a great way
to begin. **SO LET'S GET GOING!**

CHAPTER 1
WILD AND SCARY WILDLIFE

THE FEARS YOU'RE BORN WITH AND THE FEARS YOU LEARN

Some people scream at the sight of snakes and spiders. Others keep huge ones as pets and let them slither or scuttle all over them while they watch TV. Hardly anyone, however, would be happy to see a tiger or bear charging at them through a forest. And anyone who giggles underwater bubbles at the razor-filled maw of a shark clearly has something wrong with them.* There are some fears, it seems, that some folks can "switch off," while others mean "new underpants, please" for almost everybody.

So how does this come about? Are you just born afraid of certain things like sharks, snakes, and spiders? Or are you born fearless, and only later learn to be afraid as you grow up and experience scary things for yourself?

The answer is, it's actually a little of both.

Humans and other animals seem to be born with some fears, which we call inborn (or innate) fears. These include the dark, loud

* Or, perhaps, laughing gas in their scuba tank.

noises, and sudden movements. Some animals are also born with the fear of a specific predator. Mice, for example, are born fearing cats and foxes, which makes perfect sense, if you think about it. Mice born without a fear of the things that hunt them probably don't survive long in the wild. So the foolishly fearless mice have been weeded out and killed off (an example of natural selection), leaving only cat-and-fox-phobic mice behind to survive and thrive.

Similarly, many of the things humans are commonly scared of seem connected to our survival as a species. A healthy fear of thunder and lightning probably helped keep our ancestors alive during thunderstorms, as the crack and boom sent them running for cover. (Once there, they were less likely to find themselves caught out in the open—as the tallest, most zappable objects around—see page 46.) Likewise, a healthy fear of large predators (like bears and tigers) or potentially poisonous animals (like snakes and spiders) would surely have helped them survive in the wild too.

Our brains haven't evolved that much in the last 10,000 years. In fact, they're largely the same now as they were in our Stone Age ancestors. This helps explain why people living in modern cities would still be so scared of tigers and snakes, even though most of us have never even seen them outside of zoos, much less been attacked by them. In a way, our brains are wired or preprogrammed to fear prehistoric threats,

not modern ones like fast cars and fast food.

But that can't be the whole story either. Otherwise, everyone would be born afraid of the same things, and no one would be afraid of more "modern" things like airplanes and elevators, when clearly some people are. Nor would it explain more rare phobias of seemingly harmless things, like dendrophobia, the fear of trees, or alektorophobia, the devastating fear of chickens.*

In fact, beyond a few, universal fears—like the dark, loud noises, and sudden movements—most human fears are either completely learned from experience, or are developed into full-blown fears from predispositions (or fear "leanings") that we're born with. So instead of being born totally afraid of snakes, spiders, or bears, you're actually born afraid of certain shapes and types of movement. Then how you react to each animal depends on what you

* Even, believe it or not, frozen and cooked ones.

experience, and what you see and learn from those around you.

Here's how it works. Young monkeys, apes, and human children can all instantly recognize the linear, slithering motion of a snake. But how they react to it depends on whether or not the snake bites them, and how others around them react when they see one. If the snake bites, or someone around the baby freaks out, then the youngster is afraid for life. If not, they'll think of snakes as harmless until shown otherwise. Similarly, a charging bear or tiger makes a huge, fast-moving shape that will startle anyone. But children don't learn to fear bears and tigers specifically until they're attacked by one or (much more often) told that they attack people.* And right there is the key to putting the fear of a dangerous animal in its proper place. Often we develop the fear of an animal because we're told it's dangerous, because we've heard a scary story about one, or because we've seen the frightened reactions to animals of our parents and friends as we grow up. Many wild animals, to be sure, should never be messed with. But that doesn't mean they're necessarily looking to mess with us. Compared to the other dangers of modern life, very few people are ever harmed or killed by wild animals. If you understand that—plus a little about animal behavior—then you need never be terrified of an animal again.

Even the dreaded evil chicken.

---

* Think about it—ever hear the story *Goldilocks and the Three Bears* when you were little? A nasty slur on porridge-loving bears everywhere, that one . . .

SHARKS

A NAVAL NIGHTMARE

On July 30, 1945, the U.S. Navy cruiser USS Indianapolis *was sunk by a Japanese submarine near the island of Guam in the Philippine Sea. Of the 1,200 sailors on board, around 300 died in the attack, while just under 900 managed to jump overboard, with or without life vests.*

By sunrise the next day, the first sharks appeared.

At first they simply circled the survivors, who clung to each other to stay afloat. By day two, there were hundreds of sharks circling all around, and the desperate sailors—sunburned, thirsty, and exhausted—gave up any hope of rescue. Where before they shouted for help, now they fell into an awful silence.

From day three onward, the silence was broken every few minutes by a strangled scream as the sharks began to pick off the survivors, one by one. When a rescue boat finally arrived on day five, the captain watched horrified as the sharks continued to attack the men he was struggling to pull from the water.

In the end, only 317 men survived. In the worst known attack on record, a swarm of frenzied oceanic whitetip sharks had taken most of the rest.

THE FEAR Scarfed by a man-eating shark. Yikes! You don't get much scarier than that. Sharks have evolved over millions of years into perfect underwater killing machines. At one end, a mouthful of razor blades; at the other, a powerful tail that drives it through the water like a grinning torpedo . . . headed straight toward you and your failing legs. Sharks can smell a drop of blood in a million gallons of water. They can sense the electricity in your twitching muscles. And above all, they play the cello as they eat you. *Daaaaa-dum, daaaaa-dum, dum-dum-dum-dumm-daaa-dum . . .*

THE REALITY

Right? Well, not quite. Although some sharks are quite definitely dangerous animals, many are completely harmless to humans. Honest! Even the so-called man-eaters, like great white sharks, are not the bloodthirsty killers that movie directors would have us believe. And trust me, none of them can play stringed instruments. At all.

There are over 350 known species of shark. Of those, only a few—such as great whites, reef sharks, and tiger sharks—pose any threat to humans. And while it's true that these sharks do occasionally attack swimmers and divers, it's almost always by mistake. Most attacks happen to divers who try to feed or prod sharks (not very bright) or surfers who fall off their boards and onto sharks, surprising them (just plain unlucky). Unprovoked shark attacks also happen, but usually to swimmers and surfers who, to a shark, happen to look a lot like seals or turtles from below—a painful but honest mistake. In any case, once a shark has taken a bite out of a human it usually lets go and swims off rather than sticking around to chew and swallow.

Now, I know what you might be thinking. "Great—when I'm lying on the beach with my legs bitten off, I'll feel a lot better knowing that the poor shark didn't do it on purpose." But if you think about it, the idea that sharks really want to eat us is half the reason we're afraid of them. The other half, of course, is that they can and do eat us. Like, all the time. But do they?

THE CHANCES

According to the International Shark Attack File—a record of shark attacks kept by biologists worldwide—the average number of shark attacks per year worldwide is about 50. About 15 per year happen in Florida, with the rest split among Australia (6 per year), Brazil (5 per year), South Africa (4 per year), and other regions. So how many of those attacks turn out to be deadly? Well, the average number of shark-attack deaths each year in Florida is zero. Yep—fifteen bites, no deaths. In other regions (where it takes longer to get from the beach to a hospital) the average might go as high as one death per year.

Just one. Now nobody wants to be that one, of course. But if you compare your chances of dying in a shark attack to dying of something else, it helps put our whole fear of deadly sharks into place.

Let's take a quick look at some numbers.

About 1,638 shark attacks happened worldwide between 1960 and 2007. Of these, about 40% (around 650 attacks) happened in the United States, which—as we've already seen—seems to be a particularly popular place for sharks to dine on us.

But the victim was actually killed in less than 1% of these attacks. In fact, fewer than 20 people have died from shark attacks in U.S. waters in the last 100 years. That's just one person every five years, despite the fact that millions of people swim in the waters off Florida and California every year.

One of the years when someone did die from an unprovoked* shark attack was 2003. One person dead, out of about 40 recorded shark bites in the United States that year. Now compare that with some of the other causes of deaths in the United States during the same year.

Not the happiest picture in the world, perhaps. But at least it tells us that of all the things we could be worrying about, shark attacks don't come very high on the list.

* We won't bother mentioning the provoked ones. Seriously, if you actually go around provoking sharks, you probably deserve whatever toothy response is coming to you.

THE LOWDOWN

So now we know a few things. We know that most species of shark don't attack people, and even those that do bite humans usually do so by mistake. We also know that even if you are bitten, your chances of survival are still good, as most shark attacks don't prove deadly. And in the bigger picture, shark attacks kill very, very few people when compared to other dangers.

On the other hand, no one really wants to get bitten by a shark. While it might not kill you, it's pretty much guaranteed not to be a fun experience. So what's the best way to avoid them? Well, all you really have to do is avoid beaches where sharks often like to hunt, and avoid being mistaken for a fish, seal, or turtle. To do that:

TOTAL NUMBER OF DEATHS IN 2003 2,448,288	
Top killers in 2003	
Heart disease, cancer, & strokes	1,399,680
Influenza and pneumonia	65,163
Motor-vehicle accidents	43,354
Firearms	28,664
Falls	13,322
Poisoning	12,757
Drowning	3,842
Other accidents	1,510
SHARK ATTACKS	1

- Don't swim or surf between dusk and dawn—sharks do most of their hunting by night, and they're more likely to mistake you for prey in the dim light.
- Avoid swimming in murky or polluted waters for the same reason.
- Don't wear shiny jewelry—it looks like fish scales when the light reflects off it.
- Don't swim with open wounds or cuts—sharks are attracted by blood.
- Stay close to the shallows, where sharks are less likely to venture.
- And above all, avoid wearing an all-in-one turtle costume. It really won't help.

FEAR FACTS:

- Sharks have been around for over 400 million years—since long before the dinosaurs even existed.
- Great white sharks are actually very intelligent and have their own personalities and emotions.*
- Sharks never run out of teeth—when they lose one, it's quickly replaced by another growing in a "backup row" just behind. An average shark may go through more than 20,000 teeth during its life.

* Which means, out there somewhere, there's probably a shy shark, an emo shark, and an evil genius shark. I'm not sure if that makes them more scary or less scary . . .

KILLER CAT'S

THE HUNTER BECOMES THE HUNTED

"Doug could tell it was coming fast, but he couldn't see it. Suddenly, the leopard exploded out of the bush only ten feet in front of them, leaping for Doug. Doug tried to raise his rifle but the speed of the cat was too great. He shot underneath the leopard as it hit him and knocked him backward. In its fury, the leopard bit down repeatedly on Doug's right hand and wrist, ripping through tendons and crippling his arm. At the same time, its back legs pumped up and down in a blur, raking Doug's belly in an attempt to disembowel him with its bladelike claws . . ."

—From *Leopard Attack* by John B. Snow

THE FEAR

Lions, tigers, and leopards could be thought of as the sharks of the land. They're clever, effective killers. They're deadly predators at the very top of their local food chain. And like sharks, they're very capable of attacking, maiming, and devouring full-grown humans.

Big cats are lightning fast and super stealthy, so few people attacked by one ever see it coming. And once they pounce, there's little hope of escape. Leopards can run up to 40 miles per hour, leap 20 feet horizontally and 10 feet vertically, and are excellent swimmers. The sheer size and power of a big cat will strike terror into anyone who sees one up close. Adult male lions reach lengths of over 8 feet and weigh over 500 pounds. Siberian tigers have been known to reach 12 feet in length and over 800 pounds—more than four times the weight of an average human male.

Oh yeah, and if you're pounced upon, you can more or less forget about trying to fight back. With one rake of razor-sharp claws or one bone-crushing bite to the neck, it's curtains for you and lunchtime for Leo. It's no wonder that some people fear these fearsome felines so much that even being stalked by a house cat will give them the heebie-jeebies.

THE REALITY

There's no denying that lions, tigers, and leopards can and do kill people. Nor are man-eating cats a problem of the past. Wild tigers alone kill between 40 and 60 people a year worldwide. In June 2004 Indian police captured three leopards that had killed more than 12 people in that month alone. And in September 2005 a pride of lions living near the Ethiopian capital of Addis Ababa killed at least 20 people (and over 750 livestock animals), causing over 1,000 people to flee their homes in terror. Even in the United States, where there are no wild tigers,* at least 14 people have been killed by tigers in zoos and private homes in the last decade.

But terrifying as these numbers sound, they don't really paint a fair picture of big-cat behavior at all. As a matter of fact, big-cat attacks on people are extremely rare, and what we think of as "man-eating" lions, tigers, and leopards are rarer still.

* There are, of course, wild pumas (also known as mountain lions or cougars) in North America. But they almost never attack people unless provoked, so we won't bother worrying about them here. Likewise, jaguars (bigger and more powerful than leopards) roam the rain forests of South America. But jaguars aren't known to actually hunt people either. So we'll give those fearsome kitties a miss too.

Like most other predators, big cats attack for only two reasons—for food, or in self-defense. Left to themselves, few will attempt to hunt and eat a person. This is partly because we humans live in packs in clustered houses and settlements, making the preferred cat tactic of "stalk and hunt" very difficult. Some of us also carry spears, guns, and other things hazardous to a stalking cat. So, for the most part, the world's big cats have figured out that hunting humans is just not worth the trouble.

That said, if they're surprised, attacked, or protecting their young, most big cats will fight back ferociously. (You can hardly blame them for that—after all, we would probably do the same ourselves in such situations.) Otherwise, if a lion, tiger, or leopard spots a person, it'll generally either ignore the person or move away, making it quite difficult to actually get close to them even if you want to.

So how do all those big-cat attacks we've already heard about happen? Well, the majority of attacks happen when people intrude on their wild territory, or when the cats are kept cooped-up in captivity—in zoos, circuses, and even people's homes—and the keepers are foolish enough to try to play with them* or feed them by hand.

There are exceptions to this, of course.

* Ever played with an overexcited house cat, and come away with scratches and bites for your trouble? Now imagine if that kitty was twice your height, four times your weight, and had two furry handfuls of razor-sharp knives rather than needlelike claws. If you still want to play with it now, then I wish you luck. Oh, and do you mind if I "look after" your DVD collection while you're gone?

Sometimes, big cats do become people killers. But this is usually because something has happened to make them become so. Tigers—the most common and successful man-eaters—usually begin to hunt people only if their regular supply of prey (like deer and pigs) has been reduced by human hunters. Or it may sometimes begin when the tiger becomes old, sick, or injured. In all these cases, the tiger is driven to hunt people out of desperation. There's no other way it can feed itself than to take what it can get, even if that means the risky tactic of hunting people.

Very occasionally, lions, tigers, and leopards can become unusually unafraid of people and start to hunt them on purpose, preferring them to other prey. But these rogue "killer cats" are the rarest type of all, and they're most often hunted down before they can do too much damage. It's fair to say that humans don't make up a regular part of the big-cat diet, and the average person has far more chance of dying after falling out of bed than he does of becoming lunch for a lion, tiger, or leopard.*

THE CHANCES

If you don't live in India, Africa, Southeast Asia, or any other place where big cats still run wild, you're basically talking about getting mauled or killed by an escaped or captive animal. By far the most captive cats are kept in the United States, where there are actually five or six times as many tigers kept as pets than there are left in the wild worldwide. Even there, only one person

a year is killed by a big cat—almost always a zookeeper or a misguided pet-tiger owner, rather than a random, unlucky person on the street. So outside of the Asian jungles and African plains, your odds of death-by-big-kitty are less than 1 in 3 million.

If you do live in wild big-cat territory, then your chances are, of course, quite a bit higher. But even then, your odds are much better than they used to be. While tigers currently kill around 50 or more people a year in India (about half of them in the Sundarban forest region, on the border between India and Bangladesh), around a century ago over 1,000 people per year were being killed. Unfortunately there are a few places in Africa and India where lion, tiger, and leopard attacks are increasing, partly as a result of overpopulation, deforestation, and people settling within big-cat territories. But for the most part the number of big-cat attacks is dropping, along with the number of cats themselves.

* And you'd have to be really unlucky to fall out of bed and onto a lion, tiger, or leopard. Although this is another great argument for not keeping them as pets.

THE LOWDOWN

As a rule, big cats don't usually seek to attack people, and would much rather avoid human contact given the choice. When they're not given the choice, they do, occasionally, become dangerous man-eaters. But these cases are very rare, and even if you're out on safari in Africa or India, you're extremely unlikely to be attacked, since they only really hunt people whom they find alone and helpless, rather than whole groups of people in jeeps.

If you are on a trip like this, then you can stay safe by simply staying in your vehicle. Every year at least one idiot tourist has a close encounter with a lion because he or she decides to get out and take a photograph.*

Lions, tigers, and leopards, being cats, are also very curious. So if you're camping out in big-cat territory, it's not a good idea to leave your tent or hut door open at night—unless you want to wake up nose-to-whisker with a surprised carnivore four times your size.

Take these precautions, and there's little to fear from big cats, even in big-cat territory.

In fact, we humans are far more of a danger to big cats than they are to us. Fewer than 3 in 1,000 tigers become man-eaters, yet the total number of tigers left in the wild worldwide is less than 7,000. This is mostly due to hunting and habitat destruction by humans. The South China tiger, the Amur leopard, and the Asiatic lion are all either critically endangered or on the verge of extinction.

So if anyone should be afraid, it's not us, it's them.

RAWR!

* Use a zoom lens, genius—it's much easier and much safer.

MY "KILLER CAT" EXPERIENCE

When I was about five years old, my family lived in a house in Kent, England, with a huge backyard full of apple trees and gooseberry bushes. I'd often sneak down to the gooseberry bush and pick the sour green berries before they were ripe, and give myself a stomachache eating big handfuls of them.

One day, I was deep in the gooseberry bush picking berries when a cat leaped onto my head from above. It was a neighborhood tomcat—big, but certainly no tiger or leopard—and it had apparently mistaken my mop of hair for a bird. (Either that, or it was psychotic. I never did find out which.) The cat pounced and landed on my head with all four paws, piercing my scalp with its sharp claws and hanging on as I jumped up and cried out in panic for my dad.

My dad was in the yard too, building a new wall for the patio. So there he is, happily laying bricks, when all of a sudden his five-year-old son runs screaming toward him, his face streaming with blood, and a furry cat-shaped hat perched on his head.

The cat and my dad locked eyes. The cat seemed to realize its mistake and made a run for it. My dad picked up a house brick and ran after it, hurdling garden fences in his bright blue socks and jeans as he ran. In anger, but not really meaning to hurt the cat, he threw the brick. It missed the cat by approximately 50 feet (and 90 degrees) and instead smashed into a glass aviary in which one of our elderly neighbors kept his collection of pet birds. The birds flew everywhere. The old man shouted, "Oy!" My dad offered a breathless apology. The killer cat was long gone.

A few days later an old lady who lived at the end of the street came to the house with a box of chocolates. The killer cat was hers. By now, all the neighbors had heard about the killer cat attack and the crazy birdhouse-destroying, fence-hurdling bricklayer, so she had come to apologize for her cat's behavior. "He's never done anything like that before," she said.

We all felt guilty that this poor little old lady should feel so bad. After all, it wasn't her fault, and it wasn't really the cat's fault either. He just thought he'd nabbed the biggest bird in cat history. Still, I didn't feel guilty enough to refuse the apology. Or the chocolates.

BEARS, WOLVES, AND DOGS

PLAYING DEAD DOESN'T WORK

Bears, it's said, are almost doglike in their behavior. They're curious and intelligent, yet moody and unpredictable. In Canada and the United States, there are countless stories of bears attacking hikers and hunters, yet few can offer any helpful advice of what to do if you encounter one. Some say "climb a tree," yet most bears are very good climbers. Some say "run," yet a bear can hit speeds of 30 to 35 mph at a full charge. Others say "curl up and play dead," yet at least one bear-attack victim tried this and found herself bitten through the shoulder and shaken like a dog's toy. Sadly, in the powerful jaws of the world's largest and smartest carnivores, playing dead just doesn't work.

THE FEAR

The fear of dogs is called cynophobia, and it's far more common than the fear of their larger, more ferocious cousins: wolves, hyenas, and bears. But in all these cases, it's pretty much the same thing people are afraid of. It's not the bark or the howl . . . it's the bite.

Picture this: a snarling, drooling muzzle wraps around your leg, and terrible yellow fangs tear lumps of flesh from your bones. Then it snaps again at your arms, your throat, or your face.

Not scary enough for ya? Then try these little snippets for size.

FEAR FACTS:

- Enraged grizzly bears can charge, attack, and kill even after being shot three or four times (the bullets often do little to stop them—they just seem to make the bear angrier).
- Hyenas have jaws so powerful that they can crush bones in a single bite, and they've been known to attack African villagers asleep on the ground outside their huts, biting their faces right off.
- Wolves attack in pairs or packs, tearing their victims to shreds. And many of their tamer relatives are quite capable of doing the very same thing. Although we've come to love dogs as companions and guardians, pet dogs bite literally millions of people every year. Which kind of makes you wonder if that whole "man's best friend" thing is right after all.

THE REALITY

Fearsome as they are, bears—like most wild animals—very rarely attack people unless they're startled, cornered, provoked, or defending their young. So, for the most part, all you have to do to avoid a bear attack is make sure not to do any of those things when hiking through bear country. And since bears usually try their hardest to avoid people anyway, this is generally quite easy to do.

Although they have fairly poor eyesight, bears have excellent hearing and a keen sense

ACK! ACK! ACK!

Domestic dogs, however, are another story. Experts estimate that around 8% of all dogs will bite somebody during the course of their lives. How dangerous they are depends on the breed, where they are when you encounter them and—perhaps most of all—how they've been trained and treated. Some dogs are pretty much harmless. Others are very loving with their owners, but nasty and aggressive with everyone else. Still others are a danger to anyone they encounter. The trick is in telling the difference, and not doing things that provoke dogs into attacking.

All dogs are territorial animals, and most dog attacks happen in the owner's home or yard rather than out and about. Dogs kept chained up are also more likely to bite than those on leads or running free. This shows that most attacks happen when the dog feels trapped, cornered, or defensive of its own turf.

Toddlers under four are the most common age group for dog-attack victims. This is partly because they tend to approach dogs with flailing limbs and sudden motions (often pulling and grabbing at the ears, tail, or fur of the "nice goggie" as they investigate it). And although dogs of any breed can bite or attack if provoked, most of the fatal attacks come from some of those dog breeds that are bred specifically to be ferocious fighters or guard dogs, such as pit bulls, rottweilers, and German shepherds.

of smell. So they will usually amble away before you can get within a half mile of them. This makes your chances of spotting one—let alone wrestling one—pretty slim in the first place. Even if you are lucky (or rather, unlucky) enough to stumble upon one, most will just growl or pretend to charge at you in an effort to get you to back off and leave them alone. If you do the right things when this happens, you should be able to do just that—retreat and escape unharmed.

As for wolves and hyenas, they're mostly scavenging hunters that take advantage of the weak. They very rarely attack healthy, moving humans, as we seem too strong and too much trouble. Despite the wolf's "big, bad" reputation, there are hardly any reports of hyena or wolf packs attacking and eating living people.*

* Although, being efficient scavengers, many wouldn't think twice about scarfing you if they found you lying dead or unconscious somewhere. This is what happens when hyenas bite people sleeping outdoors in Africa. "Hey," they think, "maybe this guy isn't using his face anymore. Waste not, want not . . ."

THE CHANCES

While minor dog bites are fairly common worldwide, serious dog attacks are far less common, and deaths from dog attacks are very rare. In the United States, for example, there are roughly 4.7 million dog attacks per year, meaning that about 1.5% of the population will be bitten by a dog during a single year. But only around 6,000 (0.1%) of these attacks require a trip to the hospital, and only 30 or so (or 0.000006%) result in death—usually of a toddler or an elderly person. Overall, your chances of being attacked and killed by a dog are less than 1 in 150,000.

Grizzly bears and brown bears kill an average of two unlucky people per year, while the less aggressive black bears score just one. As for deaths related to wolves and hyenas, the annual average is almost zero. Because of this, weighing up the odds of being attacked and killed by a bear, a wolf, or a hyena is difficult, but it's probably many millions to one.

GRRRRR

THE LOWDOWN

Very few of us will ever come across a wolf or hyena outside of a zoo, and since attacks from them on people are so rare anyway, we can pretty much stop worrying about them right now.

Bears, however, are quite widespread in parts of North America, northern Europe, and northern Asia. Even so, the chances of being attacked and killed by a bear are still very small, and if you treat bears with caution and respect, your chances become even smaller. This includes doing the following:

- As a rule, avoid encountering a bear wherever possible. (This might sound obvious, but many a hiker has been attacked because he or she spotted a cuddly looking bear in the forest, then went in for a closer look rather than retreating.)
- Make plenty of noise as you walk through regions known to contain bears so that they can hear you coming and move away. Singing is good for this, provided it's not a Britney Spears song. This won't annoy the bear, but it may annoy your friends.
- If you do accidentally find a bear (or a bear finds you), then identify yourself as human by talking loudly and waving your arms. If the bear charges, don't run—most charges are "fake outs" that stop short of hitting you, and the bear will often move off once he's made his point. (Besides, you'll never outrun a bear anyway, and running might even encourage him to chase you.)
- If that doesn't work, you have two choices: play dead or fight back. Playing dead can work if the bear is being defensive, but if it's looking at you as food, your best chance is to fight. And your best weapon is—believe it or not—a can of chili-pepper spray. These bear-repelling sprays fire a cloud of stinging gas over 25 feet, targeting the bear's sensitive nose. In tests, it has been found to be close to 100% effective, and is a far better option than guns or kung fu . . .

As for dogs, well, they're everywhere. But again, dog attacks (especially fatal ones) are extremely rare, and a few sensible measures will help you avoid becoming a victim of the few "bad apples" in the doggie barrel.

- Don't approach and attempt to pet a strange dog unless invited to by the owner, and even if you are invited, always allow the dog to approach and sniff you first before shooting out a hand to scratch and pat it.
- If you're in a dog's (or rather a dog-owner's) home or yard for the first time, be especially wary of approaching the dog before you're sure the dog is at ease. (It should go without saying that climbing into a strange dog's kennel while making cat noises is a big no-no.) Look for warning signs, like low growls or the dog purposely holding its head level with the body (as opposed to lower or higher)—this can signal an angry dog, so it's best to leave it alone.
- If the worst happens, and you feel you are about to be attacked, there are still things you can do. Stay calm, don't run, and turn sideways to the dog, while avoiding eye contact. In dog language, this tells the dog you're not threatening it, while also not submitting to it. Usually the dog will lose interest after a bit of barking and posturing, and you can back slowly away from it.

Do all this, and your chances of being attacked—which are already very small—are much lower, and you can start to enjoy being around dogs rather than afraid of them. For the most part, dogs are loyal, friendly companions. Treat them carefully and kindly, and there's little to fear from them.

SNAKES AND SPIDERS

FANGS FOR THE MEMORY

"Like still-frame images, I remember looking at my hand after feeling an unusual and slightly painful sensation. The sight of two holes oozing blood and urine-colored venom sent my heart well into my throat.... I could already feel a numbing in my lips, head and arms, and each step I took got clumsier and clumsier.... Swallowing became a challenge. My vision distorted, making the world look as if I were viewing it from behind a dusty windshield."

From "I Should Be Dead," by Peter Jenkins

THE FEAR OK, in the Top 10 Terrifying Animals list, we've now reached the two chart-toppers. The fear of spiders (arachnophobia) and the fear of snakes (ophidiophobia) are easily the most common animal-related fears. The fear of snakes, in particular, seems to be shared across all the cultures and peoples of the world. Even in places like the Arctic, where there are no snakes at all and no one has even seen a snake before, the native people are still wary of snakes when first introduced to them by others.

And why not? I mean, when one bite could lead to terrible pain (not to mention swollen and paralyzed muscles, internal bleeding, blood clots, kidney failure, heart attack . . .) doesn't it make sense to run screaming from every snake or spider you see?

THE REALITY

Well . . . not really. Most snakes and spiders aren't venomous at all, and even the venomous ones aren't as dangerous as they seem. For the most part, anyway.

Of the 2,500 to 3,000 species of snake on the planet, only around six or seven hundred (20–25%) are actually venomous, and only a third of those (including cobras, rattlesnakes, adders, kraits, vipers, brown snakes, and taipans) are capable of killing with a single bite.

"Oh, great," I hear you say. "Only 25 percent? That's just wonderful." But if you think about it, this means over three-quarters of the snakes in the world pose no threat to people whatsoever.

What's more, just because a snake is venomous, that doesn't mean it likes to bite people. Most snakes—venomous snakes included—will try to avoid biting people where they can, and, if possible, avoid interacting with people altogether. Snakes are actually very shy creatures, and the vast majority of bites happen to people who try to catch, handle, or kill them. Even when cornered or threatened, many "deadly" snakes will give you easy-to-spot warnings before striking out—signs like rearing up, flattening their heads, and hissing and "feinting" with pretend strikes to scare you off. Spot these signs and step out of range (most snakes can only strike within a distance equal to half the length of their bodies), and you're safe.*

---

* This is not, however, an encouragement to try and guess how long a dangerous snake is, and then dance around it in a circle roughly half that snake-length away chanting, "C'mon then, snakey! Gimme yer best shot!" Humans are notoriously bad at judging lengths and distances correctly by eye. And no self-respecting cobra will let you get near it with a tape measure—so don't try that either.

FEAR FACTS:

- While most snakes have teeth, only venomous snakes have fangs. Some snakes have hinged fangs that fold back and up against the roof of the mouth, but swing forward and down just before they bite.
- All snakes are carnivores and swallow their food whole. Snakes eat everything from insects, rodents, and birds to turtles, pigs, and small deer.
- The smallest snake in the world was recently discovered on the Caribbean island of Barbados, and measures less than 4 inches in length. It has been nicknamed the microsnake.
- The largest snake in the world is the Asian reticulated python, which reaches up to 50 feet in length. The South American giant anaconda is a bit shorter, at around 30 feet, but is much thicker and heavier, with some weighing almost 500 pounds!

As for spiders, there are over 40,000 known species, yet fewer than thirty have venom that can cause serious illness in humans, and only a few (including black and brown widow spiders, funnel-web spiders, and Brazilian wandering spiders) are capable of killing with a bite. This is because spider venom typically works only on the animals (usually insects, but sometimes birds and small mammals) that the spider preys on. So most venomous spider bites cause, at worst, minor illness in humans and other animals not part of the spider's diet.

In fact, most of the spiders people think are "deadly" aren't even that dangerous. A bite from a tarantula, for example, is very painful but certainly won't kill you. A bite from the brown recluse spider may look nasty, as it causes the flesh around it to rot and die, but there hasn't been a single confirmed death from one of those either.

Even black widows, which do have the ability to kill us, hardly ever succeed in doing so because they rarely inject more than a tiny amount of venom per bite. Add to that the powerful antivenins (medicines which work against the venom of specific spiders and snakes) that are kept in hospitals to treat black widow bites, and the result is that the death rate has fallen to just one or two people per year, worldwide.

And just like snakes, most spiders are not aggressive and prefer not to get close enough to humans to bite them. In fact, most spiders are even less keen on biting than snakes, and only bite if picked up, prodded, or squashed. No venomous spider will charge or jump at you to bite, like they do in horror movies. Almost all spider bites happen when people put on gloves, footwear, or other clothing in which the spider was resting. And think about it—if you were stuck in the toe of a giant boot, and a huge fleshy foot came down to squash you, what would you do? Everything you could to stop it, I would think. And that's all poor spidey does.

THE CHANCES

So what are your chances of being killed by a deadly slitherer or scuttler?

Well, despite the unwillingness of most snakes to bite people, between 3 and 6 million people manage to get bitten by snakes every year, with over 90% of these bites typically happening in central Africa, India, and Southeast Asia.

But still, only 0.01 to 0.02% (1 or 2 in every 10,000 bites) result in death. So even if you are bitten, the average odds of surviving are over 99.98%!

For spiders, the number is a bit trickier to work out, as the vast majority of spider bites are never treated in hospitals or reported to spider researchers. But look at it this way— no spider species in the world is known to

FEAR FACTS:

All spiders have a pair of hollow fangs, which they use to inject venom into prey, but most are unable to pierce human skin with their bite.

All spiders are carnivorous (meat eaters)*, and they prey mostly on insects like flies, moths, mosquitoes, and ants. But some prey instead on frogs, lizards, snakes, birds, and other spiders.

There are two basic kinds of spider venom—neurotoxic and necrotic. Neurotoxic venoms affect the nerves throughout the body, causing muscle cramps, paralysis, and (very occasionally) death. Necrotic toxins destroy skin and muscle cells, causing blistering and blackening of the area around the bite. Snake venom can contain a combination of both of these types, and may also contain hemolytic toxins (which destroy your blood cells) and anticoagulants (which stop your blood from clotting).

The smallest spider in the world is the Samoan web-building spider, *Patu marplesi*, which measures just a hundredth of an inch across. The largest is the South American Goliath birdeater (a type of tarantula), which can be almost 12 inches across.

* Except one recently discovered species, which turns out to be a vegetarian. Weird.

HELP!

have a bite that kills over 10% of its victims. In Australia, where perhaps the most species of venomous spiders live, there have been no recorded deaths from spider bites (of any kind) since 1979. Brazilian wandering spiders,* which are thought to have the most powerful venom of any spider in the world, have caused only a handful of deaths in over 7,000 recorded bites. So these days, spiders—even the "deadly" ones—really aren't a major threat to us humans at all.

THE LOWDOWN

Spiders and snakes, basically, get a bad rap. Our fear of them is deep because it goes way, way back—perhaps to the time when our primate ancestors used to sleep on forest floors or up in trees, where they encountered spiders and snakes more often.

At least part of our fear of them seems

to be inborn. We know this because when monkeys, apes, and human toddlers are shown snakelike shapes, they spot them and react to them very quickly, even against a background of other similar objects. This suggests that humans (and some other animals) are naturally wary of snakes and spiders.

This is possibly because that very fear helped their ancestors to survive. While snake and spider bites rarely kill modern humans, it would have been a different story for our animal ancestors. One painful, swollen bite to the hand or foot could have stopped them from hunting.

That would have made even nonlethal snake and spider bites deadly in the long run. So nature would have filtered out those among our ancestors who were too curious, too unafraid, and too easily bitten, leaving only the successful snake-and-spider-phobes

* This spider gets its name from the fact that it leaves its web to wander the forest floor in search of prey. Not because it gets lost a lot and scuttles around looking confused, perhaps holding a tiny map between two of its eight legs.

behind. But when you look at it, we really don't need these fears anymore. Very few snakes (and hardly any spiders) pose a threat to us now, and they're generally easy enough to avoid, since we no longer have to go rooting around in the jungles and forests where most of the venomous ones live. If we don't meddle with snakes, then they'll generally leave us alone. And if we can tolerate having spiders around, they actually do us a favor by removing mosquitoes, flies, and other bothersome insects as part of their daily diet.

If you do come across a strange spider or snake, and you're unsure if it's dangerous or not, then dealing with it is simple. Just leave it alone, or, if it's in your house, call a vet or professional animal handler to come and remove it for you. Remember, very few people get bitten by snakes or spiders at all, but most of the ones who do get bitten were trying to catch, handle, or kill them at the time. Snakes and spiders very rarely strike . . . unless they're striking back.

If snakes or spiders genuinely give you the creeps, you may never be happy having them in your house or feeding them crickets while you curl up on the sofa. But that doesn't mean you can't share the planet with them. Even life of the slithering and scuttling variety deserves our respect and protection.

So no more washing that spider down the drain, please. Just trap him in a cup and toss him outside instead. There. Doesn't that feel better?

BEES, WASPS, & CREEPY-CRAWLIES

BEE AFRAID, BEE VERY AFRAID

The Asian giant hornet (Vespa mandarinia) is, technically, the world's largest wasp. At 2 inches long, and with a wingspan as wide as your palm, it looks more like a small bird than an insect. Until, that is, you spot the yellow-and-black-striped coloring, or the 0.2-inch-long stinger. Being stung by one feels like having a small nail driven into you, as the potent venom it injects begins to eat away at the membranes of your skin. What's more, it can fly at up to 25 mph, and it regularly attacks humans.

THE FEAR

Bugs. Creepy-crawlies. Ugh! Scuttling, biting, stinging insects have a special place in the world of animal fears. While not everyone is actually afraid of them, most of us are wary of at least one type of insect, and maybe more. And the thought of being covered in swarms of them only multiplies the imagined horrors in your head. Don't believe me? OK, try this one for size . . .

Picture in your mind, as clearly as you can, playing outside in a park on a warm summer's day. A friend kicks a ball toward you, but it misses, strikes a papery nest in a tree just behind you, and within seconds your head is surrounded by a thick cloud of angry, buzzing wasps, jabbing you over and over with their vicious, painful stings.

Or how about this: Out camping near the edge of a wide, rocky desert, you slip your bare legs into your sleeping bag and suddenly find it filled with scuttling cockroaches . . . or centipedes . . . or scorpions . . .

Yep. Creepy-crawlies got their name for a reason. They give most people the creeps.

THE REALITY

As with snakes and spiders, most insects aren't much of a threat to us at all, and yet we freak out at the sight of them through a combination of instinctive and learned reactions. Because they scuttle and buzz so quickly, their quick, erratic movements can sometimes set off our startle reflexes, making our heart rate rise and breathing quicken. But that just means we've noticed them, and if we didn't hear all sorts of horror stories about bug bites and bee stings, then most of us wouldn't be anywhere near as wary of insects as we are. After all, for the most part insects are very helpful to us, and practically none of them are actually what we'd call "dangerous."

For starters, unless you're allergic to them, no bee, wasp, or hornet on the planet can kill a human with a single sting. The average honey bee would have to sting you over 10,000 times to even get close, and since each bee dies after one sting, that's not likely to happen unless you belly flop onto a hive and roll around on it.*

What about killer scorpions? Well, again— not really. Like their spider cousins (spiders and scorpions fall into the same class of animals, called

---

* Not smart. Don't try. Period.

arachnids), the venoms of most scorpions only affect the bodies of the insects they prey on. Plus, they usually paralyze rather than kill. In humans, scorpion stings usually cause little more than a bit of swelling and numbness. Even those, like the deathstalker,* that are capable of killing people rarely inject enough venom to actually kill a healthy adult human. In fact, almost all scorpion victims are either very young, very old, or very sick. As for the other venomous insects—like fire ants, blister beetles, and a few types of hairy caterpillar—some of them could certainly make you ill, but none of them could actually "do you in" with their bite or sting.

The only real danger we face from insects (except maybe ticks and mosquitoes—but more about that in a minute) comes from being allergic to them. If you're allergic, then harmless bites and stings can quickly turn into life-threatening conditions. If you do have such an allergy, then fearing bites and stings is understandable. But it's also worth bearing in mind that most allergies are very specific—so you might be allergic to bee stings, but not wasp or hornet stings. Plus, with treatment at a hospital, even very nasty allergic reactions can be controlled if they're handled quickly.

THE CHANCES

Unless you're allergic to them, the odds of being killed by a wasp, bee, or hornet sting are around 1 in 6 million—in other words: extremely, EXTREMELY unlikely. If you are allergic, the odds are much higher, so you really do need to be careful around them. (Each year, allergic reactions to bee stings kill more people than spider bites and snakebites put together.) As for ants, beetles, scorpions, and most other insects, your chances of being seriously harmed by one of those are practically zero.

---

* Which is also, without doubt, the animal with the coolest, scariest name in the world. If a bunch of deathstalker scorpions formed a rock band, they'd just use their own name. You can't beat that.

THE LOWDOWN

Like it or not, insects are here to stay. There are between 10 million and 30 million species of them worldwide, and five out of every six animals found on land is an insect. They were here before us, and they'll probably be here long after we're gone. So we're going to have to learn to live with them. The good news, as we've seen, is that very few insect species can do us any serious harm through bites and stings, and almost none of the insects we see creeping, crawling, and buzzing around us are dangerous in any way. So hooray for the friendly bugs!

In fact, the only truly dangerous insects are ones we can hardly see, with bites we can hardly feel. Ticks and mosquitoes can be a real danger to human health—not because their bites are venomous, but because they carry with them dangerous microorganisms that can cause deadly diseases. Ticks can spread Lyme disease and the brain disease encephalitis, while mosquitoes carry diseases that include malaria, dengue fever, yellow fever, and many more.

Happily, you can actually avoid being bitten while in areas where ticks and mosquitoes live and breed. All you have to do is wear clothing that covers your arms, legs, and head; use a good insect repellent; and check yourself for unwelcome hitchhikers when you return from a hike through swamps, fields, or forests.*

As for bees and wasps, if you're allergic to stings, then you definitely want to avoid being stung (and even if you're not allergic, it's still a good idea, as it's never pleasant)! To do that:

- Don't wear perfumes or scented lotions if you're heading outside—bees and wasps may confuse them for flower scents. Avoid picking flowers or walking barefoot in the yard when bees are busy pollinating nearby.
- If you find a nest near the house, don't go near it. Call someone to relocate or dispose of it safely.
- Keep sweet fruits and soft drinks covered up, or leave them indoors. Strong sugary scents will bring wasps from miles around.
- With a few exceptions, insects aren't just safe, they're overwhelmingly helpful** little creatures for us to have around. They help maintain our environment by gardening for us (pollinating flowers, eating plant pests and weeds), they dispose of animal droppings, they nourish the soil, and they provide us with honey, silk, dyes, medicines, and more. Without them, our world wouldn't be a very nice place to live. So start thinking about them that way, and let's all try to get along, OK?

---

* I recently found a tick on the back of my neck after a short hike in the woods close to where I live. By the time I finally felt it and plucked it off, it had guzzled several times its own weight in fresh blood, and looked quite pleased with itself. In the end, I decided to throw it outside on the grass rather than kill it. Luckily for the tick, my motto—like my blood type—is "B positive."
** Yep, even wasps. They not only pollinate flowers, but they also kill pesky flies and crop pests. So they're not all bad!

THE HORDE OF HORRIBLE HORNETS

When I was about thirteen, my parents, my brother, and I drove from England to northern Italy, where my sister had been living and working for the previous two years. We stayed in a converted farmhouse surrounded by a vineyard—all yellow stone, thick wooden doors, and beautiful trees, vines, and flowers. One night, around dusk, my brother and I were sitting outside with our sketchbooks. Trying to be all arty, we decided to sit and draw the flowers in a bush right outside our open front doorway. After about half an hour of sketching, what looked like two or three small birds arrived and started hovering around the flowers. They had fat yellow-and-black-striped bodies and eyes that seemed to glow in the dark.

"Look at those hummingbirds," said my brother. "Nice, aren't they? You don't get those in England."

"You don't get hummingbirds like those anywhere," I replied. "Those things are . . . big wasps or something."

"Nahh," said my brother, "no wasp is that big . . . unless it's a hornet. But . . . nahhh, they're not that big either, are they?"

"I'm not sticking around to find out," I replied, and slowly rose from my chair, backing through the door, and keeping both eyes on the hornets in case I had to run for it. Eventually I turned and legged it into the living room.

"Dad! Dad! Hornets outside!" I yelped. "Really humongous ones!"

"Nahhhhh," said my dad, sounding exactly like my brother, "you don't get hornets in Italy."

He went to investigate anyway, taking his glass of beer with him. My brother, meanwhile, had decided that his "hummingbirds" just might be hornets after all. There were more of them now—maybe ten or twenty. So he picked up his drink and backed slowly toward the door, as I had before him.

Just as he was turning away from the hovering hornets, a vine growing across the door brushed his arm. He yelped, thinking that a stray hornet had attacked him, and in one twitchy reflex flung his drink down the hallway. My dad, seeing this, roared with laughter, calling my brother a "big girl's blouse," and pushing past him to see the hornets he was so sure did not exist.

Then he saw them.

"Bloomin' 'ell!" he said, and quickly retreated toward the doorway. What happened next was pure comedy genius. Brushing against the same vine that had spooked my brother, he too yelped and threw his drink down the hallway. My brother and I laughed until tears streamed down our cheeks. Eventually my dad joined in.

The next day we told the owner of the farmhouse, and he called out somebody to find and remove the nest. "If a couple of those stung you, you'd be in the hospital," he said. He was probably right, but, to be fair, they hadn't tried to sting us, and I don't think they would have even if we had decided to stay put instead of running. So now when I think of hornets, I laugh rather than cringe.

YIKES!

CHAPTER 2
NATURAL DISASTERS

BIG + UNEXPECTED = SCARY

Why is it that some things seem so scary that just thinking about them can make you frightened? If you've never experienced an earthquake, never seen a tornado, and never been struck by lightning, why would a gentle tremor or a distant rumble of thunder make you jumpy? And why is it some people hardly seem to notice these things while others tremble and cry out?

The answer lies in your head. Or, more specifically, in your brain.

Fear, in a sense, comes in two parts,

both of which are triggered and created inside your brain. The first part is the emotion of fear. The second part is the feeling of fear.

But hang on a minute—aren't emotions and feelings the same thing? Well . . . not quite.

An emotion is actually a series of changes that occur in your body.

RUMMMMMBLE

These changes usually happen as your body responds to something it has just sensed (seen, heard, smelled, touched, or tasted). Happiness, for example, could be triggered by the sound of birds chirping outside your window or the taste of chocolate on your tongue. The most obvious change this causes in your body is smiling.

Surprise and disgust are emotions too. They might be triggered when, for example, you slip and fall on the street. This might cause your eyes and mouth to snap open—physical changes that come with surprise. Then, as you see the squashed slug on your shoe, your mouth might narrow and turn down at the edges. This is a physical change linked to disgust.*

The emotion of fear, however, involves different physical signs—like sweaty palms, widened pupils, and a quickened heartbeat. As fear builds, it might make you tremble, freeze, faint, or even lose control of your bladder or behind muscles. How far it goes depends partly on how big the trigger (or stimulus) is that starts it off. So just as

eating a slug might trigger more disgust than slipping on one, a deafening crack of thunder will trigger more fear than a gently popping balloon. But it also depends on how unexpected the stimulus is. That's why popping a balloon yourself is far less likely to scare you than having someone sneak up and pop one right behind your head.

Does all that sound a bit obvious? Well, if it does, then hold on—because that's only half the story.

Aside from the emotion of fear, there's also the feeling of fear. While an emotion is a series of changes that occurs in your body, a feeling is how you experience and

* Interestingly, most people tend to say "uuuuuuuuuuurrghh!" in this kind of situation too—a word that seems to mean "That's surprisingly revolting!" in almost all known languages.

explain those bodily changes in your brain. The feeling of fear is actually created in a different part of the brain than the emotion of fear (the emotion in the center, the feeling kind of around the outer edges and toward the front), and this is part of the reason why different people respond differently to the same "scare triggers" or stimuli.*

When it comes to being big and unexpected, you don't get much bigger or more startling than natural disasters, like storms, tornadoes, and earthquakes. So for all of us, these are pretty big triggers for the emotion of fear. But just because they're big, powerful, and (let's face it) dangerous, that doesn't mean we need to live in fear of them. For starters, the chances of getting hit by a lightning bolt or tornado are pretty

small in most p
where huge sto
common, there
avoid them, ma
safer.

The differe
and being unaf
of how much y
you are. If you
earthquakes wo
deal with them, then you can change how you feel about them and cope much better with the emotions of fear that they create. You can actually use the logical, thinking part of your brain to partly override the emotional part.

Everybody experiences the emotion of fear, but how we feel fear is up to us.

---

* Stimuli, by the way, is the plural word for stimulus, just as fungi (rather than funguses) correctly describes a bunch of mushrooms. Confusingly, the plurals of octopus and platypus are not octopi and platypi, but octopuses and platypuses. You can blame the Greeks for this. I always do, anyway.

THUNDER AND LIGHTNING

LIGHTNING ON THE LINE

"No one ever told me you weren't supposed to be on a land-line telephone during an electrical storm. So, there I was, calling in a takeout pizza order, when I noticed that the lightning and thunder was getting more intense, and coming more frequently. Then I heard static on the phone line, which kept getting louder and louder. Then I heard what sounded like a loud explosion, and at the same time I noticed a bright, white light at my feet, which was football-shaped, and had spikes. It blew me across the floor, and I was knocked out for a few seconds.

"My son came running into the kitchen, to find me laying there on the floor."

Lightning survivor "Missy," the United States

THE FEAR Astraphobia, or the fear of thunder and lightning, is one of the most common fears in the world. And for good reason—lightning is truly terrifying stuff. At over 54,000°F, a bolt of lightning is five to six times hotter than the surface of the Sun. Each bolt moves so fast that not even a ninja could dodge it. A single lightning strike contains over a billion volts of electricity at a current of up to 160,000 amperes. That's enough to power a lightbulb for over three months, and 2–3 million times more powerful than it needs to be in order to kill you.

Lightning doesn't play fair either. It can rip through buildings and vehicles, and it can hit whole crowds of people at once. If the main strike misses you and hits something else, it can "splash" from nearby objects and zap you anyway, or travel through the ground and hit you from the feet up. Even if it misses you entirely, the shockwave caused by the exploding air around it can knock you flat, break your ribs, and burst your eardrums. And what if it struck while you were flying in an airplane? Would the plane explode or fall out of the sky? If it hit your speeding car, would you be blown off the road? And if it can even hit you indoors down the telephone line, then surely there's no escape! Gaaaaaaagh!

THE REALITY

OK, so there's no getting around it—lightning is definitely very dangerous stuff. Triggered by a buildup of charged particles within massive clouds, a bolt of lightning literally rips the air apart as it goes, traveling at over 136,000 mph and reaching temperatures hot enough to melt iron. No one wants to mess with that.

That's part of the reason why we (like most other animals) have evolved to be jumpy at the boom and flash of thunder and lightning. It's a pretty healthy fear to have, and one that has kept us and our animal ancestors alive for thousands of years. The huge noise, temperature, and electric current that come with lightning can trigger a very strong fear response. But knowing a little more about how lightning works can help us keep our reactions to lightning under control.

There are several types of lightning, including cloud-to-ground (CG), cloud-to-cloud (CC), in-cloud (IC), cloud-to-air (CA), and ball lightning. But all of these only happen within (or around) a certain type of cloud—the thundercloud, called cumulonimbus. The cumulonimbus is a huge, dark, towering monster of a cloud, so it's pretty easy to spot and avoid. And simple as it sounds, that's pretty much all there is to it: avoid being out in a thunderstorm, and you have very little to fear from lightning.

This is because lightning, or at least the cloud-to-ground type that poses a threat to us, only really wants to do one thing—connect a thundercloud to the ground (through the air) so that it can release its built-up electric charge. But since air doesn't conduct electricity too well, lightning usually (but not always) strikes the tallest thing around in an effort to avoid traveling through too much air. That's why it often hits tall towers, buildings, and trees—the towering wood, metal, and concrete structures give the electric charge an easy path to the ground. This is easier than if it had to travel through more air to flow through objects or people closer to the ground.

This is also why it's generally safe indoors during thunderstorms. If lightning does hit your building, then it already has a nice, easy path to the ground through the walls (especially if they contain metal pipes or electric cables), so why would it force its way through the air inside just to hit you and your friends? Of course, if you offer it a new path to you through a telephone cable or a gadget plugged into a socket, then you're asking for an indoor zapping . . .

The same goes for cars and airplanes, which are both—as a matter of fact—quite safe places to be when lightning strikes. The cagelike metal structure of cars usually channels the electric charge safely around the passengers inside, leaving them totally unharmed—although it may melt the tires, knock out the electrical systems, and stop the engine. Airplanes, in a sense, are even safer. They're specifically built to channel lightning strikes around the passengers and fuel tank, through the use of metal shielding in the outer skin and walls. In fact, lightning strikes airliners all the time, but the passengers rarely notice!

KRAK!

THE CHANCES

The odds of getting hit by lightning vary, depending on where you live, how many thunderstorms that area gets, and how much time you spend outside. So it can range from about 1 in 80,000 (highly unlikely) to 1 in 400,000 (almost never gonna happen). But your odds of being hit are hugely affected by how you behave during storms.

Lightning kills about 10,000 people a year worldwide—more people each year than tornadoes, flooding, or any other kind of bad weather. But it's worth noting that almost all of these people were outside in a thunderstorm at the time, many of them working in fields, hiking, fishing, boating, playing golf, or running around on open sports fields. Remove these "extreme farmers and sports fans" from the figures, and fewer than a couple hundred remain (which in a world of over 6 billion people ain't too bad). Less than 1% of lightning victims are hit indoors, and most of those are on the telephone at the time (a good reason to stay off the phone during storms too).

BOOM!

THE LOWDOWN

So in short, lightning is scary stuff, but you don't have to be afraid of it as long as you stay smart and stay safe. In fact, as long as you respect it and take a few precautions, you're pretty much in the clear. Knowing that (and perhaps telling yourself that as the storm rumbles and flashes on) is the first step toward changing how you feel about thunder and lightning. You may still get tense and short of breath (signs of the emotion of fear) when the thunder first cracks, but knowing how lightning works and behaves can help you control the feelings that follow, so that the fear gradually ebbs away.

Of course, knowing what to do during a storm will make you feel even better. And for the most part, that means calmly seeking shelter at the first rumblings of a thunderstorm. Don't wait for the rain, since lightning can sometimes strike ahead of the downpour. If you like, you can count the time between each thunderclap and lightning flash to work out how far off it is—just divide the number of seconds by 6, and you get the rough distance away (in miles) of the center of the storm (so 30 seconds = 5 miles). But do this indoors. Then stay indoors until the storm has passed. Many lightning strikes actually happen at the edges of the cloud, making the beginning and end of a storm the most dangerous parts. You think, "It's not here yet," or, "It's gone" . . . then BOOM!

If you're outside fishing, boating, or playing sports, stop and go inside. Remember, being "macho" or "extreme" about lightning is the best way to end up as one of those 10,000 actual annual lightning victims. Finally, realize that "take shelter" doesn't mean "stand under a tree." Quite the opposite, in fact.

While the tree will shelter you from the rain, it may attract a lightning strike, and you're likely to be hit along with it.

If you really can't get in out of the storm, conventional wisdom is that you should crouch down in a ball and hug your knees. That way, you make yourself as small a target as possible, and if the lightning does strike you, it should flow quickly from your head/neck to the ground—hopefully avoiding causing serious burns and nerve damage on the way through. But this really is a last resort and shouldn't be relied on. Even taking these precautions, if you are struck, you're just as likely to end up looking like a charred pebble as you are to escape unscathed.

One last happy fact to think about: believe it or not, lightning victims usually don't die. About 70–95% of the time they survive, often with just a few burns and scrapes.

Still—wouldn't want to try it, eh?

FEAR FACT:

Jet airliners are struck by lightning, on average, at least once a year, every year. So a single jumbo jet may be hit thirty times or more during its normal lifespan of 100,000 takeoffs and landings!

TORNADOES, BLIZZARDS, AND SANDSTORMS

HIT BY A TWISTER

"The roar of the storm grew louder. Windowpanes were cracking. Wind was blowing throughout the living room. Dishes, pots, and paper were flying from the kitchen. Plaster was crumbling away from the walls. My mother Zena, my brother Gordon, and myself were on the first floor of the farmhouse when the tornado hit us. The roar was like a freight train. As the walls collapsed around us, knocking us down, we happened to fall beside the dining room table. It was an old wooden farm table, and it made a tiny space and barely held the walls from crushing us. My brother Tom was upstairs in his bedroom. He pulled the covers over his head. As the house collapsed, Tom's bed flew, and he wound up in the front yard."

Survivor of the 1953 Beecher Tornado, Michigan

THE FEAR

Few people like the idea of being engulfed by roaring, deafening winds and tossed around like a rag doll. Fewer still want to be buried alive in sand, snow, or bits of their own house. Desert sandstorms can blind or suffocate people. Violent snowstorms, called blizzards, can freeze you to death with their icy winds and leave you buried beneath several feet of snow. And perhaps most frightening of all is the terrifying, concentrated power of the tornado, or "twister." Twisters can strip the bark off trees, turn cars into flying missiles, and flatten entire towns. You'd have to be crazy not to be even a little bit alarmed by that.

THE REALITY

Happily, sandstorms and blizzards aren't nearly as threatening as they seem—at least for most people on the planet. Formed by natural (but powerful) shifts of air between areas of high and low pressure, they're little more than strong winds carrying sand or frozen water.

Both tend not to happen outside the desert or snowbound regions where people expect them to be. And even when they do surprise the locals, both types of storm are quite survivable. If you're caught outside in a sandstorm, a wet cloth over the nose and mouth will stop you from choking on grains of flying sand, while proper cold-weather gear will insulate you and stop you from freezing to death in a blizzard. Prepared like this, you can usually seek shelter or higher ground before the sand or snow has a chance to bury and suffocate you. For the most part, sandstorms and snowstorms only pose a threat to travelers in remote areas, or to people cut off from food, water, or power by drifting sand dunes and snow outside their houses. So if you live in the desert, on high mountains, or in the Arctic, you'd better be prepared. If you live elsewhere, don't sweat it—you're safe!

Tornadoes, on the other hand, are much more dangerous and far more frequent. Caught out in the open by a full-force twister, there's little to do but pray for a soft landing (and that's if you haven't already been peppered by bits of flying car and house). Some places—such as the famous "Tornado Alley," running from Texas in the south to Nebraska in the north—do get more twisters than others. But tornadoes actually appear quite regularly on every continent in the world, except Antarctica.*

---

* Which is almost a shame, since an Antarctic tornado would at least give penguins a chance to see what flying is like.

The good news is that the vast majority of tornadoes aren't killers. Most don't even cause much damage beyond a few broken tree branches and toppled chimneys.

Tornadoes are measured on the Fujita scale (named after Tetsuya "Ted" Fujita, the Japanese professor who created it), which goes from 0 to 5, based on the amount of damage the twister does. F0 and F1 ("weak") tornadoes snap branches, peel off roof shingles, and shift cars around in driveways. F2 and F3 ("strong") twisters uproot trees, topple trains, and tear roofs off houses like lids off yogurt cups. By the time you get to F4 and F5 ("violent") tornadoes, you get flying cars and farm animals. You also, occasionally, see houses lifted right off the ground, then broken into pieces that land hundreds of yards away.* Which, among other things, really confuses mail carriers.

Perhaps not surprisingly, F4s and F5s cause most (roughly 67%) of the deaths and injuries associated with tornadoes. But thankfully they're also by far the rarest type of tornado, which keeps the flying-house traffic down to a happy minimum.

THE CHANCES

The odds of dying in a sandstorm or snowstorm are, for most people, very low— perhaps 1 in 1 million. Of course, if you're crossing the Sahara or Gobi Desert by camel, or trekking through the Himalayas, then your odds are a lot higher. But then, if you're the type of person who does those kinds of things, you're either very well prepared, or you're that Bear Grylls guy on TV. (And if things go bad for him, he can always eat the guy with the camera.)

Tornadoes are a bit easier to stick a number on. Of the 1,000 or so tornadoes that strike the United States (the most twister-prone region of the world) each year, only 1% are F4 or F5 "violent" ones, and that low percentage seems to hold true for the rest of the world too. As with lightning, your chances of being hit by a tornado also depend on where you live. The average odds of experiencing death-by-twister sit at roughly 1 in 60,000, but are much lower outside tornado-prone regions.

* Or, if your name is Dorothy and you're in the movie *The Wizard of Oz*, it might deposit you, your dog, and your entire house in another dimension—surprisingly all in one piece.

THE LOWDOWN

Sandstorms and snowstorms are dangerous, but fairly predictable. You may never see one in your little part of the world, and, even if you do, they're not so hard to deal with if you're properly prepared.

Tornadoes, however, are famously unpredictable, and there's no real way to "deal" with them apart from getting out of the way or hiding somewhere safe. To that end, people who live in areas where twisters are common often build underground storm shelters, or take cover in the basement of the house when a tornado warning is sounded. It's also important if you live in a "twister zone" to keep an emergency survival kit handy (with food and water, flashlight, radio, and first-aid kit) in case you get trapped inside the house. The most important thing, though, is simply to stay aware of what's going on with the weather, so you know if it's likely that a storm will bring tornadoes along with it. That means checking the TV and radio weather reports whenever there's a storm around. Meteorologists (scientists who study weather patterns) can predict where and when tornadoes are likely to appear just by watching for spinning cloud patterns within storms. And although they're not always right, it pays to listen to them, just in case!

Scary as all this sounds, there is a happy ending. Thanks to improvements in weather-forecasting methods and communication by TV and radio, the number of deaths caused by "killer" tornadoes has been dropping steadily in most parts of the world. In the United States during the 1950s, 18 tornadoes killed more than 18 people each. In the 1980s, only 2 tornadoes killed that many, largely thanks to the better warnings and information people were receiving by then. So while twisters can be fearsome, we don't need to feel too afraid of them if we understand them and do the right things. If you're still not sure what these things are, check out this handy tornado guide:

TORNADO'S and TORNADON'TS

DO	DON'T
Listen for tornado warnings on TV and radio during storms.	Listen to your iPod or watch *Twister* on DVD.
Prepare an emergency kit, just in case.	Prepare your hang glider.
Take cover in the basement if a tornado is coming. If the building you are in doesn't have a basement, try to find a room—such as a closet or bathroom—that doesn't have any walls that are external to the building.	Sit on the roof with your digicam and try to get some good shots for YouTube.

HURRICANES AND SUPERSTORMS

THE WRATH OF KATRINA

On August 29, 2005, Hurricane Katrina, one of the most devastating hurricanes of all time, slammed into the southern coast of the United States. Over the next two days it tore through Louisiana, Mississippi, Alabama, Tennessee, Kentucky, and Ohio, leaving a trail of floods and damaged buildings 125 miles wide. Worst hit was the port city of New Orleans, where winds hit speeds of over 125 mph, and floodwaters surged over the protective barriers north of the city, leaving 80% of it underwater and destroying over 200,000 homes.

All told, Katrina caused more than $125 billion worth of damage, eclipsing Hurricane Andrew's $21 billion wrecking spree in 1992, and making it the single most destructive hurricane in recorded history. Yet in terms of human losses, neither could compare to the Galveston hurricane of 1900, which killed more than 6,000 people and completely destroyed the coastal island of Galveston, Texas. Of this, one Galveston reporter said that the events of September 8, 1900, "could never truly be written. As for many, no words could ever be spoken again about the deadly hurricane that reshaped the Gulf coast forever."

THE REALITY

Tropical storms—and their larger cousins, typhoons, hurricanes, and cyclones—are no joke. The average hurricane measures around 340 miles across and releases more energy in 24 hours than all the power plants on the planet put together. To make matters worse, superstorms like these bring with them a hat trick of dangers: winds of up to 150 mph, high waves and storm surges, and flash flooding caused by heavy rain. OK, now for the bright side. Only about one-third of the tropical storms and cyclones that strike land each year are what we'd call major storms, or storms in categories 3, 4, or 5 on the Saffir-Simpson hurricane scale. These are storms with wind speeds of over 110 mph and are the ones that commonly

STORMS, CYCLONES, AND HURRICANES

STORM	A disturbance in the Earth's atmosphere that affects its surface—usually through strong winds, heavy rain, and possibly thunder, lightning, ice, snow, or hail. They can be light, moderate, severe, or extreme, depending on the wind speed.
CYCLONE	An organized, rotating storm system that forms over tropical or subtropical waters. There are various types of cyclone, which are given different names depending on which ocean they form over. To be a true cyclone, the wind speed must be over 74 mph.
TROPICAL CYCLONE or CYCLONIC STORM	A cyclone that forms over the Indian or southwest Pacific Ocean.
TYPHOON	A cyclone that forms over the northwest Pacific Ocean.
HURRICANE	A cyclone that forms over the Atlantic or northeast Pacific Ocean.

EVACUATION ROUTE

destroy buildings and cause dangerous flash floods. The majority of tropical storms fall into categories 1 and 2. These have winds between 74 and 100 mph. So they're still very powerful, but they usually do little more than fell trees, break windows, and flood roads. In the last 100 years, there have been only a handful of category 5 storms, so the worst kinds of superstorms are fairly rare.

Even if a major storm does hit, the winds rarely knock down entire houses, and with proper hurricane-proof windows, shutters, and roof supports on your house, wind poses little danger to anybody inside.

The real danger comes from the heavy rains, storm surges, and flooding. These do pose a real threat and tend to cause almost all the deaths during major storms. So that's where you need to act fast in order to stay safe. Tropical storms and hurricanes are enormously powerful, but they're also huge and fairly slow moving, so they're reasonably easy for weather forecasters to spot and track. The best way to avoid the dangers of a hurricane is to simply not be there when it hits. If you pay close attention to weather reports and leave at the first sign of trouble, there's nothing even a superstorm can do to harm you.

THE CHANCES

The odds of being killed in a superstorm (including being struck by the hail, lightning, and tornadoes that accompany it, or drowning in floodwaters) are roughly 1 in 50,000. Again, this varies a bit depending on whether you live near the coast or inland, and whether or not you live in an area prone to hurricanes and typhoons (like the southeastern United States or southwestern Japan). But the real risk has more to do with how much information about approaching storms you have access to, and how quickly you can evacuate if you need to. With good advance warning and plenty of time to escape, you can reduce your odds of being hurt in a superstorm to almost zero.

THE LOWDOWN

Superstorms will probably always be a threat to people living in many areas of the world. But although they may regularly destroy buildings and property, they can be spotted, tracked, and avoided by people, given enough of a warning. Storm-tracking radar and computer software are becoming more powerful and accurate all the time. And armed with the knowledge they give us, we can beat a respectful retreat from superstorms without having to live in fear of them. As with other types of natural disaster, you can also prepare for the worst by strengthening your house, preparing an escape route, and putting together an emergency survival kit—just in case you're unable to get away from the house in time. With all this done, your odds of being harmed by a superstorm go from "very low" to "extremely low," and you can feel confident and prepared rather than anxious and afraid.

I experienced my first superstorm in Japan in September 2000. I had moved to Japan in July of that year, just one month before the start of the official "typhoon season"—the two months when most of the typhoons happen. Growing up in England, I'd never really experienced a hurricane or typhoon before. (There was a small category 1 hurricane in Kent when I was 12 years old, but I slept right through it and woke up confused to find my parents walking around with candles because the power was out!) So when this first typhoon hit the city of Tsukuba, where I was out food shopping that afternoon, I completely underestimated it. As I emerged from the shopping center, hundreds of Japanese shoppers were gathered by the door, afraid to go outside as the wind roared past. "It can't be that bad," I thought. "Besides, I have to get this ice cream home before it melts." So, ignoring the other shoppers' protests, I pushed past them and stepped out into the typhoon. Bad move.

Tables and chairs from a nearby café whipped past my head. Bolts of lightning struck things within a hundred yards of where I staggered and leaned into the wind. I got less than half a mile away from the shops before the deafening thunderclaps scared me into a sprint, and I ran (still trying to keep hold of my shopping bags) to shelter in a nearby hotel. A uniformed security guard inside called to me and pulled me into the hotel lobby: "Gaijin-san! Hayaku! Kochi! Kochi!" ("Quick, Mr. Foreigner! In here! In here!"). He must've thought I was a complete loony.

I waited there for an hour and a half while the typhoon passed, then finally set off on the rest of my journey home. As I neared my apartment building, I found a pair of my pants lying damp and sodden in the road. Then another. Then a T-shirt and a single, lonely sock. All mine. Unfortunately I'd left all my washing out to dry on the balcony of my third-floor apartment, and the typhoon had helpfully distributed it all over my neighborhood.

Oh well. At least I still had the ice cream . . .

VOLCANOES, EARTHQUAKES, AND TSUNAMI

MOUNT ST. HELENS EXPLODES

At 8:32 a.m. on May 18, 1980, an earthquake of magnitude 5.1 occurred directly underneath the volcano. This was the trigger for the enormous eruption that quickly followed in its wake. Within a few seconds, the entire north flank of the mountain exploded, creating one of the most gargantuan* rock and debris avalanches of all time, advancing at a speed of 60 mph. Within seconds, the temperature in the danger zone had soared to over 570°F. Snow and ice on the peak of Mount St. Helens melted instantly, creating raging torrents that poured down the slopes into the valleys, destroying all life in their path.

* If you haven't seen this word before it means "really, massively, hugely enormous." As opposed to the massively, hugely annoying "ginormous," which isn't a word at all, and really bugs me. Why glue "gigantic" and "enormous" together, when either one can do the same job just fine on its own? Might as well say "egantic." Pah!

THE FEAR Smothered, burned, and melted by a river of red-hot lava. Crushed inside a crumbling building, or thrown into a deep crack in the earth beneath your feet. Flattened and drowned by a colossal tidal wave.* Not many of us have experienced an earthquake, tsunami, or volcanic eruption—but not many of us would want to either. The deadliest earthquake on record killed over 830,000 people in Shaanxi, China, in 1556. And in 2004 the deadliest tsunami on record killed over 225,000 people in Indonesia, Thailand, and Sri Lanka.

As for volcanoes, about fifty or sixty erupt every year. Half of them just spew molten lava down their sides, while the other half actually explode—sending out huge, deadly clouds of gas and rock, and raining down lava bombs and thick, suffocating ash for miles around.

Scary? Errr . . . yes.

THE REALITY

Volcanoes are essentially holes in the Earth's outer crust, through which red-hot, molten rock (magma) from the liquid layer beneath can escape. If the molten rock oozes its way out gradually, you get bubbling lava flows, and the cone of a volcano is built up from layer upon layer of this stuff setting hard on top of itself. But if the route to the surface becomes blocked by hardening magma, it "caps" the volcano, and pressure can build up beneath until it eventually blows its lid. This is what happens during a volcanic eruption.

An erupting volcano is an awesome and hellish sight, and you certainly wouldn't want to be anywhere near one when it goes off. Just ask the people of Pompeii, Italy, who until AD 79 lived on the sides of an active volcano called Mount Vesuvius. When Vesuvius blew, it buried the town in clouds of burning ash, leaving little behind but statuelike impressions of the poor townspeople and their pets.

Now, you might think to yourself, "Why would anyone want to risk living on the side of a volcano in the first place? The people of Pompeii were just asking for it, weren't they?"

Well, as it happens, the soil around volcanoes tends to be very rich in nutrients and ideal for farming, so many towns and villages have been built on the slopes of volcanoes to take advantage of the fertile ground. And as risky as this "extreme farming" might seem, the people who choose to live this way know something else about volcanoes too—that the chances of actually being killed by one drop steadily the further you are away from the crater. And while you may think, "Great—then I'll stay at least a thousand miles away, thanks!" for

---

* Not that "tidal waves" have anything to do with tides. They're caused by earthquakes or (every 100 million years or so) asteroid strikes. Another egantic failure to use the right words. Oops. Now I'm doing it. Let's stick with the term "tsunami."

many volcano-dwelling farmers, the risk is worth the reward. Here's how it works.

At less than 300 feet from the crater, you're in the death zone. Here you have extreme temperatures, mini-earthquakes, landslides, toxic gases, and virtually no chance of survival in the event of an eruption. So staying here for long pretty much guarantees you'll be toast.

At 300–1,000 feet away, you've got roughly a 50% chance of surviving an eruption, provided you're not hit by the pyroclastic cloud—a plume of boiling gas and rock that explodes out of the crater at temperatures up to 1,400°F. If that happens, you may have the rare honor of being vaporized—turned into a gas—yourself.

At 1,000 feet to 6 miles away, you're still at risk from lava bombs and mudflows, but your odds are getting better. Particularly if you're good at dodgeball and swimming.*

At over 6 miles away, you're actually fairly safe. Although lava flows may travel further than this (60 miles or more, sometimes), lava isn't, believe it or not, that much of a danger to people. It usually moves very slowly (2–3 mph), so you can walk backward faster than it flows toward you. Look at it that way, and it doesn't seem quite so scary, does it?

As for earthquakes, they're a bit different. Earthquakes are caused by floating plates (called tectonic plates) of the Earth's crust grinding past each other. All the continents and oceans of the world sit on top of these vast plates, and in turn, they sit

(or rather "float") on top of a sea of molten rock in the mantle layer beneath. The plates and the landmasses on top of them are constantly moving. We usually don't notice this because they move too slowly for us to feel it. Except, that is, during an earthquake.

During an earthquake, the grinding plate edges (plate boundaries) can become temporarily stuck or caught against each other. Pressure and strain build up between the two surfaces—until eventually the tension breaks and the plates jerk free. This sudden jolting movement creates the

* OK—this is a lie. No one's that good at swimming. Or dodgeball.

massive vibration that we—sitting on the landmasses above the plates—experience as an earthquake.

The good news is that while small earthquakes are very common (about 8,000 per day!), on average we get only one very large quake (scoring 8 or more on the Richter scale) each year, worldwide. Also, the big, damaging quakes almost always happen in specific, predictable areas—on the boundaries between the floating tectonic plates we were just talking about. Some regions (like Japan, Indonesia, northern India, and the west coast of North America) sit right on top of a plate boundary, so they get more than their fair share of large earthquakes. Other regions (like northern Europe, Australia, and central Africa, and the Midwestern United States) sit right in the middle of a plate, so they get very few. So depending on where you live, you might not have much to fear from earthquakes at all.

Tsunami are almost always caused by large earthquakes, but are rarer still. They happen as an undersea earthquake sends a sudden ripple of motion upward through the water from the ocean floor. This ripple lifts a vast ridge of water above the sea surface, which then collapses into a series

TSUNAMI HAZARD ZONE

IN CASE OF EARTHQUAKE, GO TO HIGH GROUND OR INLAND

of immense waves that grow larger and larger as they approach shallower depths near land.

They're also only really a threat to people living in low-lying coastal areas or islands, and if you live far enough inland (or up high enough) they won't really affect you. And even in the areas that are threatened, the prediction and warning networks for tsunami have improved a lot in recent years. This now gives people more of a chance to escape in the interval between the earthquake and the wave hitting land.

THE CHANCES

The odds of being killed by a volcanic explosion, lava flow, or associated mudslide are about 1 in 80,000. Obviously they're much higher if you live right on the side of a volcano, but, on the flipside, if you live nowhere near a volcano, your odds of being killed by one pretty much drop to zero.*

The average person stands a 1-in-130,000 chance of dying in an earthquake, and only a 1-in-500,000 chance of being killed by a tsunami. Again, this changes a lot depending on where you live. But for most people in most places, it's highly unlikely that you'll be hurt by either one.

---

* Unless, that is, a massive supervolcano like the one under Yellowstone Park, Wyoming, blows. Then we could all be done for. But thankfully that happens only about once every million years or so. The last super volcanic eruption was about 75,000 years ago, so we should be fine for a little while (or 925,000 years) yet. Phew!

THE LOWDOWN

If you live very close to a volcano, close to a plate boundary or on low-lying coastline in a region known for earthquakes, then you need to be aware of the risks and dangers of eruptions, earthquakes, and tsunami. Just as with hurricanes and tornadoes, a little preparation and planning can go a long way toward keeping you safe in the event of a disaster. Usually this just means knowing how to get to a safe place quickly and having food, water, and emergency supplies ready in case you're trapped or stranded.

But if the place where you live doesn't fall into one of those three categories, then you have little (if anything) to fear from these three forms of natural disaster. Thankfully, geologists and engineers have learned a lot from past earthquake experiences, allowing us to build more earthquake-proof buildings in cities and towns near plate boundaries. These structures are designed to bend and sway during an earthquake, rather than crack and crumble. So if you live in one of these, there's far less chance you'll become trapped or injured inside. We've also become a lot better at monitoring plate boundaries and volcanoes for signs of trouble, which helps us to predict (although far from perfectly) where and when earthquakes, eruptions, and tsunami are likely to happen.

Sure, it's possible that a large earthquake might happen right in the middle of a plate . . . that a tsunami might travel farther across the ocean and farther inland than usual . . . or that an unknown underground chamber filled with magma might erupt without warning and form a new volcano in your hometown. All of these things are possible. But the chances of them actually happening are so small that they're basically not worth worrying about. As we'll see in the next section on asteroids and comets, some things have such frighteningly huge consequences that they're hard to ignore. Yet once you know the massive odds against them, ignoring them is exactly what you can and should do. Volcanoes, earthquakes, and tsunami are big and scary, certainly. But if they still freak you out, just ask yourself:

What are the odds?

FEAR FACTS:

Volcanoes can be classified as active, dormant, or extinct. Active volcanoes either erupt regularly or still show signs that they might erupt again—like swelling, shifting, or regular earth tremors. Dormant volcanoes have been quiet for at least 10,000 years, and extinct volcanoes are unlikely ever to erupt again—usually because their underground lava supply has been cut off.

There are about forty known supervolcanoes in the world. These are volcanoes that have produced particularly (and frighteningly) large eruptions in the past—eruptions big enough to blast out a crater 40 or 50 miles wide and affect the entire Earth's climate as exploding gases enter the atmosphere.

Almost all supervolcanoes are extinct. The last one to blow was Mount Toba in Sumatra, roughly 75,000 years ago. That eruption was ten thousand times more powerful than the Mount St. Helens eruption in 1980.

Not long after my first typhoon experience in Japan, I soon had the pleasure of my first real earthquake. I was sitting in an Internet café, e-mailing a friend back in Scotland, when the earthquake hit the building (well, it actually hit the whole city and surrounding area—but you know what I mean). It started with a gentle rumbling and rocking of the room, and I thought at first it was maybe just a big truck going by. But then the rumble got bigger. The floor, the walls, everything started shifting from side to side, practically scaring the pants off me. I mean, like most people who didn't grow up in earthquake-prone regions, I'd always kind of taken it for granted that floors and walls . . . well . . . stay put. Take it from me—it's very unnerving when they suddenly decide not to.

Jumping out of my seat, I quickly scanned the room to locate the exits. "But wait," I thought to myself. "Should I make a run outside to the parking lot, duck under the desk in case the ceiling falls in, or what? And what about everyone else in here? They don't seem to be going anywhere. So should I grab them and help them outside too? . . . or . . .

"Hang on a minute. Nobody else is getting up. They're just sitting there. They're still TYPING!! In fact, they don't look bothered at all. . ."

So, very slowly, and keeping an eye on all the Japanese e-mailers around me who seemed so unafraid of the continuing earthquake, I sat down again and continued my e-mail.

"Heiyyy there," I typed, trying hard to hit the right letters as my fingers skidded around on the keys, "therre seems to be amn esrthqiuake goiung onn. Nobosy else seems botherdd tho' . . ."

It was the first of many earthquakes I'd experience during my two years in Japan. None of them did anything worse than tip bottles, glasses, and books off shelves, and although none of them turned out to be dangerous, it took a long time before I stopped freaking out whenever they happened. The weirdest thing was suddenly waking up in the middle of the night and wondering why you were awake . . . then feeling the gentle rumble and rocking of the earthquake's aftershock.

ASTEROIDS AND COMETS

A "SECOND SUN" FALLS ON SIBERIA

"We were sleeping. Suddenly we both woke up at the same time. . . . We heard whistling and felt strong wind. . . . We started crying out for father, mother, brother, but no one answered. There was noise beyond the hut, we could hear trees falling down . . . then the thunder struck. . . . This was the first thunder. . . . The earth began to move and rock, wind hit our hut and knocked it over. . . . Then I saw a wonder: trees were falling, the branches were on fire, it became mighty bright . . . how can I say this, as if there was a second sun . . . my eyes were hurting, I even closed them. . . . And immediately there was a loud thunderclap. This was the second thunder. The morning was sunny, there were no clouds, our Sun was shining brightly as usual, and suddenly there came a second one!"

—Tungus tribe witness, 1905

THE FEAR

On June 30, 1905, an asteroid or comet exploded 5 miles above Tunguska, a remote forest area in Siberia, Russia. The words on page 62 come from a witness to the event, a child of one of the Tungus tribes that lived in the area. Although no one is known to have died from it, the Tunguska fireball flattened 1,200 square miles of forest, and was the largest asteroid or comet impact in recorded history. But that's not to say that bigger ones hadn't happened before . . .

The Tunguska asteroid was just 200 feet across, yet it exploded with the force of 1,000 atomic bombs. A strike from an asteroid ten times larger would cause earthquakes, throw up enough dust into the atmosphere to blot out the Sun, and kill millions of people worldwide. If it were ten times larger again (about 4 miles wide), the explosions, earthquakes, and firestorms that followed would most likely make us extinct, along with most other species of life on the planet. This is called an Extinction Level Event (or ELE), and it's thought that this is what killed most of the dinosaurs—along with 75% of the Earth's other species at the time.

If an asteroid or comet of that size hit us again, we'd have nowhere to run, nowhere to hide. We'd be done for. No question. So in the grand list of things to be terrified of, surely this has to come near the top, right? Right?

THE REALITY

You probably didn't know this, and you might not believe it, but huge rocks from space are thumping into Earth's atmosphere all the time. And not only do they regularly fail to wipe out the human race, but most of them go completely unnoticed.

Unless, of course, you're a stargazer. Or, better yet, a shooting-star gazer. That's because space rocks measuring less than a few feet across usually burn up in the atmosphere, causing pretty, flashing meteor trails—also known as shooting stars. If they're a bit larger, they might cause small, temporary fireballs that disintegrate long before they hit the ground. And while a huge planet-killing fireball is a truly terrifying thing to think about, asteroids hundreds of yards across (and capable of causing an ELE) don't strike Earth very often. If they did, then we probably wouldn't even be here, as it would've been difficult for life on Earth to get a foothold with pesky fireballs destroying most of it every thousand years or so.

The last really big one was probably the same one that finished off most of the dinosaurs. It struck Earth around 65 million years ago, and the chance of one that big hitting us again within the next century is less than one in a million. The same goes for comets, which are more or less the same thing as asteroids, only they're more ice than rock.

Of course, some rocks do sometimes make it all the way down to the ground (those are the ones we call meteorites). Even some pretty large ones. So there is an outside chance that one of these might crash through the ceiling of your house while you're in the shower, or drop out of a blue sky while you're out for a relaxing stroll. But the chances of one falling right where you are at the time are incredibly small, so smaller meteorites don't pose much more of a threat to you than their larger asteroid cousins.*

THE CHANCES

In all, the odds of being killed by a falling space rock (including meteorites, asteroids, and comets) during your entire lifetime are between 1 in 200,000 and 1 in 500,000. This is regardless of where you live, or how much time you spend looking up in an effort to dodge them. This also makes space rocks—believe it or not—one of the least hazardous natural disasters around, so they're not really worth worrying about at all!

* As a space rock, you don't get to be called an "asteroid" unless you're at least 98 feet wide. So I imagine there are lots of very miffed 97-foot rocks out there in space, who probably still tell all their friends they're "asteroids, really."

THE LOWDOWN

The odds of being struck, individually, by a single falling space rock are so small that most people rightly ignore the possibility of it—in much the same way as they ignore the possibility of a satellite, an airplane, or an unlucky skydiver falling on them.

These things seem so unlikely they're almost funny to think about. But massive, planet-killing asteroids are different. When you hear about them, they conjure up images and words—explosion, firestorm, extinction—that may trigger a real emotional response (changes in heartbeat and breathing, sweating, and so on) in your body. With that comes the feelings of dread and fear. And suddenly the risk of being killed by an asteroid seems many times larger than it actually is. But the risk hasn't changed—only how you're thinking about it.

Asteroids and comets are a perfect example of how our emotions can get in the way of our logic and reason when it comes to things we're afraid of. In effect, the emotional part of the brain decides how good, bad, safe, or scary something is before the logical part even kicks in. So you're left feeling really afraid of something, yet you can't really explain to someone else exactly why that is.

One way to break this fear cycle is to start to look at the same scary things in a new way. Weighed against other nasties, asteroids and comets are so unlikely to affect you at any time within your lifetime that it's better to think of them as "never gonna happen" and be done with it. Then, chances are, Earth will keep spinning through space largely unbattered by anything too big, and you can take relaxing strolls and showers without wearing a crash helmet.

FEAR FACTS:

There are over 100,000 known asteroids in our solar system, including 2,000 that are classed as Near-Earth Objects (or NEOs), which pass through Earth's orbital path, and have the possibility of hitting us one day.

In fact, a 197-foot asteroid called 2009DD45 whizzed past Earth on March 2, 2009, missing us by 40,000 miles. That might seem pretty far off but, in terms of space distances, it's actually a close shave.

Over 12,000 asteroids have been named, and if you spot a new one, you're allowed to name it yourself!

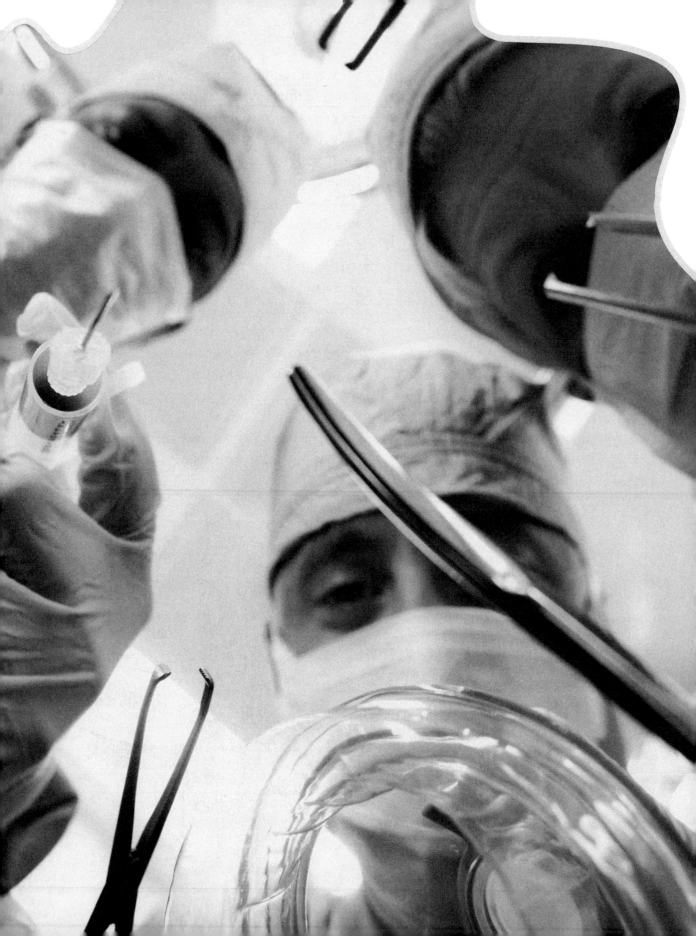

CHAPTER 3
DOCTORS, DENTISTS, AND DEADLY DISEASES

SCARY STORIES

Ever heard a horror story about an evil nurse who terrorizes people with her needles and instruments, or a dentist who seems to love causing pain?

How about news headlines like "Killer Bug Ate My Face" or "New Flu Could Kill Millions"? Chances are, you've seen or heard one of these at least once within the past year.

And barely a week goes by without there being some kind of food-poisoning scare in the news. Beef is laced with deadly *E. coli* bacteria. Chicken and eggs give you salmonella. It's enough to make you avoid going anywhere—or eating anything—ever again!

But if all these stories were really true, then surely we'd all have been done for a long time ago. Every week, stories like these appear in newspapers, on TV, and on the Internet. Yet we keep on going to the doctor and dentist, going out, eating food, and breathing air—all with few signs of these killer people and bugs we hear so much about. So what's going on?

One simple answer to that question is that many of these stories (such as the ones your friends tell you about doctors and dentists) are exaggerated or completely made up.* But they can't all be lies. I mean, newspaper and TV reporters can't just make things up and get away with it, can they?

Well, not exactly. But it's important to understand that newspaper reports, TV programs, books, and movies all need to have stories in order to be interesting. So the people who create them tend to choose subjects that will make good stories. That means something with good guys, bad guys, danger, and drama. And "killer bug" stories fit that formula perfectly.

So when some innocent, unsuspecting person somewhere is killed by a rare nasty virus—or a rare case of food poisoning—then it makes great material for news reports, and the same stories get repeated over and over again. Unfortunately for us, this tends to give us the idea that killer bugs and food poisoning are a lot more common (and a lot more dangerous) than they actually are.

This is because our brains weigh up how risky things are partly by using memory. If we can remember recently being bitten by a snake, poisoned by a bad egg, or burned by a hot pot, then our brains make us react carefully (or even fearfully) when we next encounter snakes, eggs, and pots. But if the bite, burn, or bout of food poisoning happened a long time ago—and we've safely dealt with snakes, eggs, and pots plenty of times since—then we gradually forget about these "dangers." With enough time and experience, we even begin to relax around them or ignore them completely.

The trouble is, our brains don't fully separate out the things we hear from someone else (or the things we see in newspapers, on the Internet, on TV, and in the movies) from the things that actually happen to us. So whenever you see or hear a story about an evil dentist, or a TV report about a "deadly" virus or "poisonous" egg, the brain files this idea in the form of a memory, which it may refer back to later on as if it was real.

Little by little, your brain starts to get the idea that killer dentists, viruses, and foods are all around you and killing people all the time! Your brain takes no notice of the fact that you've never actually been

---

* One of my friends in elementary school once told me that a dentist had actually killed him the day before. I stared at him for a few seconds until he realized what he'd just said. He stared back. Then he added, "Well—he didn't kill me dead, obviously. I mean, I got better . . ."

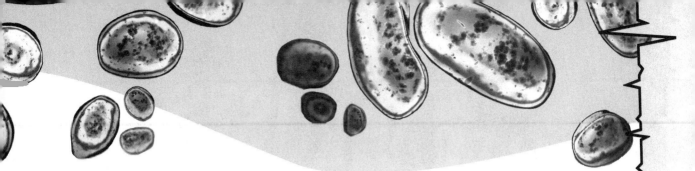

harmed by a dentist, virus, or food. Nor does it note that the dentist story may have been exaggerated or made up, or that the reports were about rare viruses and rare batches of poisoned food.

So the next time you go to the dentist, or you encounter the "killer" food, or someone sneezes near you on a bus, your brain refers to these false memories and kicks off an automatic fear response. You don't notice this happening, but it does. All you know is: "Dentists are evil," "That egg might kill you!" and "That gross snotty guy on the bus might have swine flu!"

But the truth is that doctors and dentists aren't deadly; everyday germs aren't vicious killers; and real "killer bugs" are so rare in the world that they aren't much of a danger either.

In fact, bacteria and viruses are all around us, all the time. And as long as we stick to a few simple steps in dealing with them, we certainly don't need to flinch from every patch of dirt or airborne snot-droplet that we encounter.

So without further ado, let's dive into the icky world of medicine and microbes . . .

KILLER VIRUSES INFECT THE WORLD

WORSE THAN WAR OR PLAGUE

In 1918 a great pandemic (or whole-world outbreak) of the influenza virus killed between 25 and 50 million people across the globe. This so-called "Spanish flu" killed three times as many people as the whole of World War I, which had only just ended. In fact, more people died of influenza in those nine months than in all four years of the bubonic plague—the famous "Black Death" that swept through Europe in the fourteenth century. Although far less serious, two more pandemics followed in 1957 ("Asian flu") and 1968 ("Hong Kong flu"). And in June 2009, the World Health Organization announced the first influenza pandemic of the new millennium—the dreaded H1N1, commonly known as "swine flu." Could this deadly pig plague be the Black Death of the 21st Century?

THE FEAR

Viruses like the one that caused the 1918 "Spanish flu" outbreak are still with us, lurking in pigs, birds, and other animals and just waiting for the chance to mutate and start infecting people. The influenza virus is particularly sneaky because it changes its outer appearance by mutating every time it infects a new host. This makes it one of the hardest viruses for the body's immune system to recognize and fight off, and also makes it almost impossible to wipe out with vaccines.

By the time you create a vaccine against the current form of the virus it has already changed, so the vaccine won't work—or at least won't work so well. With no effective vaccine and no cure, a new form of influenza like bird flu or swine flu could—in theory—cause even more damage than the Spanish flu did a century ago. The 1918 virus infected around a fifth of the world's population (which at the time was about 1.8 billion) and killed millions. If that happened again—in today's world of over 6.7 billion people—more than 1.3 billion would be infected worldwide. That's about equal to the entire population of China, or roughly four times the population of the USA. Yikes!

THE REALITY

Those are some scary numbers, and the truth is, a new strain of flu already has swept the world and infected millions of people—people on every continent around the globe.

But don't panic! Once again, we're only getting one side of the story . . .

Swine flu, or H1N1, as it's known to virologists (scientists who study viruses), has infected millions, but in fact, it has so far turned out to be less dangerous than the "regular" influenza viruses which sweep the world every fall/winter flu season. Of those infected with swine flu, over 90% have managed to shrug it off without needing any treatment at all. The remaining 10%—who became ill enough to be admitted to the hospital—were mostly very young children or elderly people whose immune systems were too weak to fight the virus. Of those that died (just 1-2% of those infected with the virus) most were already suffering with other, serious medical problems like heart disease, kidney failure, or severe diabetes.

So for otherwise healthy people, swine flu poses far less risk than the normal flu. And for those in more vulnerable groups—like babies, toddlers, the elderly, and people who are already weakened by other diseases—vaccination programs have been

used to hold the virus down. While not perfect, these vaccines provide enough protection to give these people roughly the same, strong fighting chance as healthy adults.

As for bird flu, the panic about that comes mostly from the fact that this strain of flu changes (or mutates) extremely quickly, making it almost impossible to vaccinate against. This also makes it very deadly to the animals it infects, as their immune systems have so little time to mount a response before it changes its outer coat to look like something else.*

Wild birds can carry the avian influenza virus in their guts without getting sick, but when it passes to domestic birds like ducks, geese, and chickens,** they often become sick and die. If that were the end of the story, there wouldn't be much of a problem. Every year some farmers would lose a few flocks, but beyond that, no danger. The trouble is, sometimes the

COUGH!

virus can mutate so that it can infect humans too. And when it does, it very often kills them. Influenza viruses that have "jumped" from birds to people have so far killed over 300 people in parts of Southeast Asia, West Africa, and the Middle East, and every year the number of people infected seems to be growing.

But this doesn't mean bird flu is about to infect the whole world. In all of the human cases seen so far, the virus was caught directly from an infected bird or from contact with bird droppings. (Part of the reason why these infections are happening is because people in those places keep live birds in crowded markets and in their homes, making it easy for the virus to spread to people. You can't get bird flu from eating chicken.)

This is important because it means the "bird" virus hasn't mutated into a "human" one, so it can't be passed between humans yet. Phew!

---

* This is a bit like the virus putting on a wig and one of those glasses-nose-moustache disguises. "Nahh—I'm not flu," it says to your immune cells. "I'm Dave. You know—Dave Harmless, from down the road. No need to worry about me . . ."
** Which I suppose might give you one good reason for being alektorophobic (see page 8) after all.

So at the moment, this flu virus is still a bird flu that can infect people who live closely with birds, rather than a human flu set to spread around the globe in coughs and sneezes.

In all, this means you don't have to worry too much about catching deadly flu strains from that snotty guy at the bus stop, or that kid who sits behind you and keeps coughing on you in class.* That's because—in short—bird flu doesn't spread among humans, and swine flu is no more lethal than "regular" flu.

THE CHANCES

As scarily widespread and common as it seems, the numbers show that swine flu isn't nearly as bad as most people think. So far, swine flu has sent a few thousand people to the hospital in Canada and America, and killed over 6,000 people worldwide. This might sound bad. But compare that with "regular" influenza, which sends an average of 200,000 to American hospitals (and claims around 36,000 lives) every year. Looked at this way, there's no reason to be any more scared of catching swine flu than you are of catching the regular kind. Taking steps to avoid catching the flu is a good idea, anyway. But unless you're in a high-risk group, swineflu isn't so different and terrifying a disease.

As for bird flu, the chances of you catching that right now are so small that it's hardly worth thinking about. Even in Southeast Asia, where the most cases of bird flu have been found, the odds are as low as 1 in 4 million. In the United States, Europe, and most other places there have been no cases of bird flu found in humans. Here the odds are more like 1 in 100 million. That makes "death by bird flu" the least likely thing in this book to happen so far!

THE LOWDOWN

Swine flu is no more deadly than your standard, seasonal flu, and for the moment, it seems to be under control. If you keep your hands clean and avoid coughing, spluttering people, that should be enough to avoid both kinds.

As for bird flu—that's different. It has the potential to be much more deadly than swine flu if it jumps to human hosts. But for now, it's only a threat to bird farmers, and even then it's more of a threat to their wealth than it is to their health. While 300 people infected with avian flu over the last few years might sound

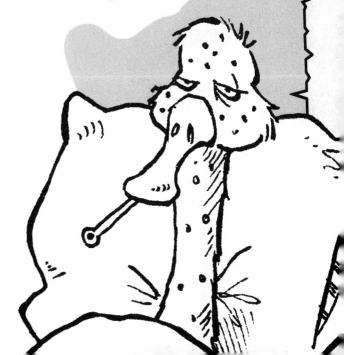

---

* Although this still isn't too cool, and you should probably ask him to cover his mouth anyway. You might not get bird flu from him, but you might catch a common cold or—at the very least—a big, wet blob of phlegm on the back of your neck. Mmmmmm, nice.

like a lot, it's almost nothing compared to the 500 million people infected with "regular" human flu each year, the vast majority of whom survive. So bird flu, at the moment, is hardly even a dot in the bigger picture of world diseases.

Of course, there's always the chance that avian influenza could mutate into a strain that can jump among humans—and if that happens there could be another pandemic like the one in 1918. But it hasn't happened yet, and it may not happen within our entire lifetimes.

If that doesn't make you feel much better, then try this: if a new flu pandemic as deadly as the 1918 one were to happen, we'd almost certainly be a lot better prepared to battle it than the world was nearly a century ago. We've already succeeded in limiting the spread of swine flu with monitoring and vaccination programs.

And even without a bird flu vaccine, we've learned so much about the spread of diseases and how to treat viral infections since then that we would most likely save millions more lives. Back in 1918, we'd barely got the hang of radio broadcasts. Nowadays, news spreads around the world in an instant via satellite signals and the World Wide Web. So governments across the globe can work together to limit the spread of disease through quarantines, instantly share information about new viruses as they arise, and airlift medical supplies and doctors in a matter of hours.

Of all the "scary, deadly" diseases that make it into media reports every month, bird flu is, in reality, probably the worst of the bunch. But the new "Black Death" is not here yet, and if we're lucky it may not come at all—at least not in the way it did back in 1918. In the meantime, scientists and governments are keeping an eye on flu outbreaks in every corner of the world . . . just in case. So when a truly deadly flu strain comes again, it'll have to face a global self-defense force. Next time, hopefully, we'll be ready for it.

FEAR FACTS:

Although people often get them mixed up, bacteria and viruses are very different things.

Bacteria are tiny living organisms—the simplest forms of life on the planet. Each bacterium is a single living cell, which feeds, grows, and splits itself in two in order to reproduce. These two "daughter" cells then split again and again, creating a colony of organisms. They live pretty much everywhere on the planet, inside and outside our bodies.

Viruses are not considered to be true living things, since they cannot feed, grow, or reproduce by themselves. Smaller and simpler than bacteria, they consist of a small strand of DNA (or a related chemical called RNA) surrounded by a protein coat. Viruses pass into living cells (either bacteria or those of other organisms) and hijack the cell machinery to copy themselves.

Antibiotics work on bacteria because they stop bacterial cells from growing or reproducing. Antibiotics don't work on viruses because viruses have different structures and ways of reproducing than bacteria. So there's no point taking antibiotics for a cold or viral infection.

DIRT, GRIME, AND BACTERIA

WORLD OF GERMS

Right now, whether you know it or not, you're surrounded and under attack. A vast, invisible army of bacteria is all around you, ready to strike from every possible angle.

Sitting outside on the freshly mown grass for a picnic? Every gram of soil beneath you contains over a billion bacteria, of over 10,000 different species. Going for a swim in the sea? The salty water contains up to 200,000 bacterial cells per gallon. And if you think your house is spick-and-span and bacteria-free . . . think again. The average home boasts 3.2 million bacteria per square inch of toilet bowl, 18,000 bacteria per square inch in the kitchen sink, 300 per square inch on the telephone, and 200 per square inch on every light switch.

THE FEAR

Germs, or bacteria, cause disease by attaching themselves to us and gaining entry to our bodies. They crawl in through our eyes, ears, noses, and mouths. They squeeze through cracks and cuts in broken skin to enter the tissues and blood vessels beneath. They even hitchhike on dust particles and water droplets floating in the air and are sucked deep into our lungs with almost every breath.

Once inside, they breed. They divide, multiply, and party. They squeeze water and nutrients from our cells, they travel around the body in the bloodstream, and they make us ill in any number of different ways.

Since bacterial germs thrive in dirt and filth, the fear of dirt and the fear of germs go hand-in-hand, and we give them a single name—mysophobia. True mysophobics will do anything to avoid getting dirty or contaminated by germs. They'll stay indoors to avoid the "filthy" world outside, open doors with their elbows, and wash their hands up to fifty times a day in an effort to stay germ-free. But with over five million trillion trillion bacteria on the planet (that's a five with 30 zeros after it), there really is no escaping the big, filthy, world of germs . . .

THE REALITY

It's true—like reality TV programs, germs are everywhere, and there's no getting away from them. But for the most part, we don't need to, as few of them do us any harm. Over 95% of the bacteria on the planet are completely harmless. Which is how all of us (and I mean all of us, not just the stinky ones who don't wash) can carry trillions of bacteria around with us every day without even noticing them.

Staphylococcus bacteria cover your skin and line the insides of your nose and mouth. Your stomach lining harbors millions of rod-shaped lactobacillus bacteria. Your guts contain billions of *Escherichia coli* (otherwise known as—gasp!—the dreaded *E. coli*). And that's just for starters. They live in your teeth, on your tongue, under your fingernails, up your rear end* . . . pretty much anywhere you can imagine. What's more, they live there for your entire life. Yet none of them (usually) do you any harm.

That's because they've evolved to live with us, and we've evolved to live with them. They've adapted to thrive at our normal human body temperatures, and to feed happily on bits of undigested food, dead skin cells, and other things we don't need. Our bodies hold them in check by using the skin and gut lining as a barrier, keeping them outside the body or inside the long food tubes of the digestive system. This stops them from

* So the next time you complain that the place you live isn't much fun, just think: it could be worse—you could be a bacterium.

77

BACTERIA ENTRANCE

GOOD GOOD BAD

getting into the tissues and bloodstream where they could do us harm.

And if they make it past that first line of defense, our immune cells race in to provide reinforcements. White blood cells and antibodies that find bacteria in the tissues or bloodstream surround them and summon help from other cells—cells that punch holes in bacteria and digest them. Like an army of microscopic bouncers or security guards, immune cells use the invading bacterium's outer coating as ID, and clone thousands of copies of "memory" cells that recognize that ID—just in case that type of bacterium tries to get in again. Those immune cells are pretty smart.

But why make it all so complicated? I mean, why don't our bodies just kill off all the bacteria and be done with it?

Well, for starters that'd be no easy task, since (as we've seen) bacteria are everywhere in our environment, all the time. So it'd be an enormous waste of energy to try and kill off all the bacteria we come into contact with, just to get at the few among them that might do us any harm. Instead, by keeping a layer of harmless bacteria around, our bodies use the "good" bacteria to keep out

the "bad" ones. The trillions of harmless bacteria that already live on us (and inside us) outcompete most of the would-be settlers that might do us harm—by eating all their food and stopping them from getting a toehold on our bodies.

Also, many bacteria are actually incredibly helpful to us in hundreds of ways. We use them to make foods, drinks, vaccines, antibiotics, fuels, pesticides, and more. As a matter of fact, we wouldn't even be here without them, and we couldn't go on living without them either.

Bacteria were the first forms of life on the planet, and they evolved billions of years before we did. They spent billions of years altering Earth's atmosphere by sucking up methane and carbon dioxide and spewing out oxygen. If they hadn't been there and done that, then none of the big, oxygen-breathing animals on the planet—including us—would ever have developed and survived. Even now, bacteria continue to remove carbon dioxide from the air and oceans. This helps provide the very air we breathe, and also helps protect us from the effects of global warming. Pretty helpful for a bunch of "killer" bugs!

THE CHANCES

Of course, bacteria and viruses can and do kill people. Common infections picked up from the environment cause an average of 35 deaths per country, per year. In some places it's much higher, in others much lower. And your chances of picking up an infection depend, of course, not only on where you go, but also what you do there. If you go for a swim in an open sewer, or roll around with your mouth open in the grassy dog-walking area of your local park, then you're far more likely to pick up harmful bacteria.* But just hanging out in the average home, yard, beach, meadow, public building, or park, you're very unlikely to be made ill by bacteria—provided you follow a few basic rules (see below). Follow these rules, and your chance of being killed by a common infection drops to below 1 in 1 million.

THE LOWDOWN

It's pointless wasting energy trying to avoid contact with germs, since (a) you don't need to because most germs are harmless, and b) it's absolutely impossible to do anyway!

Besides that, trying to keep your body and environment too sterile (say, by using antibiotic soaps or too much disinfectant around the house) might actually weaken your immune system by stopping it from being exposed to bacteria. Remember, your body's immune-cell "bouncers" need to ID the "bad guys" to recognize them and protect you in the future.

If you want to protect yourself against bacterial and viral infections, then these few basic rules should be more than enough:

- Wash your hands after going to the bathroom and before eating. This prevents you from transferring harmful bacteria from your hands to your mouth, where they may be swallowed.
- Avoid picking your nose or biting your fingernails. Apart from being gross, these are great ways for bacteria and viruses to hitchhike their way into your body on a grubby fingertip.
- If the defensive barrier of your skin is broken by a scratch, cut, graze, burn, or animal bite, always clean and disinfect the wound to stop bacteria from sneaking in through the gap.

Beyond that, you needn't worry about random germs getting into your body, as millions of years of evolution have already done all the worrying for you. Your immune cell "bouncers" are waiting at the doors, and if the bugs aren't invited to the party, they're not staying for long.

FEAR FACT:
Bacteria live in every known environment in the world. Some live their whole lives floating in the atmosphere, while others have been found living more than 4,700 feet underground. Some survive year-round in Arctic ice, at temperatures as low as −121°F. Others live inside volcanic vents in the deepest parts of the ocean, at temperatures above 223°F.

---

* Not sure why you'd want to do this, unless perhaps your dog has real trouble learning the "roll over" command and you're trying to demonstrate it for him. In any case—bad idea.

FILTHY ROTTEN FOOD

MICROMONSTER

We've all eaten something that "didn't agree" with us. Perhaps it was a slice of pizza left out too long in the pizzeria or a yogurt left too long in the fridge. Most of the time we get away with a sore stomach and a quick sprint to the bathroom. But pity the poor person who eats food containing the bacterium **Clostridium botulinum**. When this little monster disagrees with us, it really disagrees with us. It normally lives in soil, but when it finds its way into the human body through foods (usually vegetables) it causes complete havoc.

The botulinum *toxin* is the most powerful poison known to man. It paralyzes nerves and muscles, stopping you from speaking, swallowing, and (eventually) breathing. One gram of it could kill a million people, and less than a nanogram (0.000000001 g) is enough to kill a single child or adult. If there was ever a great excuse for not eating your vegetables, this is it! But since the bacterium is easily killed by washing and cooking—and eating your vegetables is better for you than skipping them—your mom is unlikely to agree. Sorry.

THE FEAR

We all have to eat, and most of us do so at least three times per day. That means eating more than 70,000 meals over the course of a lifetime, any one of which could contain a microorganism that makes you horribly ill. Some of these "food bugs" just make us feel tired or sore for a few hours. Others make us vomit and poo explosively (sometimes both at the same time). The very worst of them can paralyze and kill us, and judging by the high number of news reports we see about these food bugs, that must happen a lot.

Listeria lurks menacingly in cheese, campylobacter camps out in tainted meats and milk, and salmonella sits waiting in everything from chicken to eggs to chocolate. Food poisoning strikes millions of people every day, all over the world.

But if we have to eat to live, then what do we do when our food is trying to kill us?

THE REALITY

Don't worry—our food isn't really trying to kill us,* and neither are most of the bacteria that live in it. As we saw in the last section, less than 5% of the bacteria around us (including those living in or on our food) are actually harmful, thanks in part to the strength of our immune systems.

But it's true that some bacteria can and do cause us harm when we swallow them, and roughly 1 in 3 of us will become sick with food poisoning at one time or another in our lives. In the United States alone, around 76 million people get food poisoning each year, and these millions are matched (or topped) on every other continent (except perhaps Antarctica, where there simply aren't millions of people to get it!). Thankfully, the vast majority of these "poisonings" turn out to be pretty mild, rather than the "deadly" outbreaks we hear so much about in the media.

E. coli, for example, is usually a harmless bacterium, and billions of them live in our guts already. Millions of people eat *E. coli* along with their food every day and never even realize it. The only problem comes when a rare and dangerous type (or strain) of the bacterium turns up, like the 0157:H7 strain that causes most of the *E. coli* outbreaks you hear about in Europe and North America. This particularly nasty strain makes a toxin called the shiga toxin, which causes vomiting and diarrhea, and can be fatal. But this strain is very rare

---

* Except, perhaps, for fugu, the poisonous pufferfish eaten in Japan. That one really is trying to kill you. Specially trained chefs are supposed to cut out the poison glands before they slice and serve it, but every year at least a few people drop dead after eating "questionable" ones. I ate fugu once, without realizing what it was. Luckily I'm still here to report back on how it tasted: good, but not so good I'd risk my life by eating it twice!

(less than 1.5% of all food-poisoning cases involve it), and what's more, 90–95% of people who become ill with it survive.

The truth is that while food poisoning is pretty common, serious illness or death caused by food poisoning is pretty rare. And if you treat your food properly, by storing and cooking it carefully enough, then food poisoning is totally avoidable and nothing much to worry about.

THE CHANCES

The odds of getting food poisoning differ among different countries. In the developing world, over 1.8 million people are killed each year by microorganisms in food or water. In parts of Africa and Asia, food poisoning is a common cause of death. But these tend to be places without good water treatment, without good sanitation (sewers and waste-removal systems), and with poor hospitals and health care. In developed countries like the United States, Canada, and the United Kingdom, far fewer people are killed, although still probably more than should be—between 400 and 5,000 per year. But all in all, your chances of dying of food poisoning are still very low—probably around 1 in 3 million.

THE LOWDOWN

Food poisoning is common enough to be a real danger, but as long as you follow a few simple rules for storing, preparing, and eating your food, it's still nothing to be afraid of. Take care with your food and you can enjoy it fear-free for life.

Keeping food fresh and safe is all about preventing bacteria from growing in it, or killing them off if they already have grown. So . . .

- Make sure you store your fresh foods properly, keeping them in the fridge, or (if you're keeping them for longer) freezing and defrosting them as needed.
- Remember that chilling and freezing don't usually kill bacteria; they just stop them from growing so fast. This is why your food still "goes bad" in the fridge eventually, so keep track of how long things have been in there by checking sell-by dates and labels. This is also why you shouldn't refreeze things once defrosted—bacterial spores can survive the first freeze and multiply when they're thawed, so the second time you thaw the food it could be swarming with bacteria within minutes of defrosting.
- Make sure foods that need to be cooked—like meat and eggs*—are fully cooked before you eat them. That means heating them right through to kill all the bacteria inside, not just heating up the outside and leaving the middle lukewarm (this is especially common with fast-cooking microwave ovens, so beware!). Check the food packaging for guidelines. Once cooked, eat the food immediately, or store it as if you hadn't cooked it at all, as even within a few hours more bacteria from the air can settle and start to grow back.
- If you're eating raw foods like sushi, make sure they're ultrafresh so that bacteria haven't had hours to grow on them before you eat them. Also, keep raw and cooked food separate when preparing meals, to prevent bacteria from being transferred from one to the other. And always wash your hands after handling raw food, to avoid ferrying bacteria from your fingers to cooked foods later on (or straight into your mouth!).
- Finally, if in doubt, throw it out! If something looks or smells dodgy, then it probably is. Much safer to discard it and let the bacteria grow in the garbage can, rather than swallow it and see what happens in your stomach!

* It is possible to eat raw (or rare) meats and eggs, of course. But unless they're VERY fresh, you're always at risk of food poisoning. So if you're in any doubt, it's better to cook 'em up and show the bugs no mercy!

HOW TO EAT IN REVERSE

When I was little, I was a terribly picky eater. My mom had a lot of trouble getting me to eat vegetables. And chicken, beef, and fish had to be in the form of nuggets, burgers, and sticks before there was any guarantee I'd eat them.

But after college, and just one year of living in Japan, all my picky eating habits went out the window. I was eating all kinds of raw and cooked vegetables, and I discovered that I really liked sashimi and sushi (cuts of fresh raw fish served on their own or on top of lumps of sticky rice). These fresh, raw foods had more flavor to them, and I gradually became more and more brave and experimental with the things I ate. After the raw fish came raw shrimp, raw crab, raw jellyfish, and raw sea cucumber (which is a long warty sea worm, not a vegetable). One of my favorite things was a thin cut of nearly raw beef called shabushabu. To kill off the bacteria, you just swiped it twice through a dish of boiling water, then popped it in your mouth. It was juicy, tasty, and delicious.

Then one evening, I went out to dinner with some of the other teachers from the school where I was working. They all ordered namatori, which is, basically, small chunks of raw chicken plopped on top of a bowl of rice. But I wasn't convinced.

"Raw chicken?" I said, "Won't that make you sick?"

"No, no," answered my friend Makoto,* "It's very fresh. Like sushi. It's very good!"

So, trusting in my new "iron stomach," I ordered up my own bowl of raw chicken chunks, and (trying to ignore the fact that it looked very much like a bowl of cat food), I scoffed it down. The next day my body decided to teach me a painful lesson about bacteria and raw meat.

---

* This is the same guy who fed me the poisonous fugu pufferfish. You'd think I'd have learned my lesson . . .

Some forms of food poisoning make you throw up for hours, until your head spins and it seems like the bottom has fallen out of your world. Others leave you stranded on the toilet for hours while the whole world—ahem—seems to fall out of your bottom. This one did both.

By the end of it, I was lying in a hospital bed, dizzy and several pounds lighter, hooked up to a drip of salty fluids and vitamins through a needle in my arm. None of my friends had become sick from the namatori. They were immune, it seemed, to the bacteria which had so successfully attacked my guts for the previous 24 hours.

I still love Japanese food, and I happily eat raw fish all the time. But I draw the line at raw chicken. Unless you want to find out what it feels like to be a bubbling fountain of body fluids, I suggest you do the same . . .

NEEDLES, DOCTORS, AND DENTISTS

NEEDLE NIGHTMARE

I counted down the days on the calendar with increasing dread. A month before the jab, I imagined it as a thin, sharp, three-inch needle being stuck into my shoulder, making me yelp in pain as the nurse pushed the plunger thingy down. A week before the jab, the needle had grown in my thoughts. Now it was six inches long and looked like a steel drinking straw, and it made my whole arm go dead as the nurse cackled and jabbed it in. An hour before the jab, sitting in the doctor's waiting room, the daydream had become an epic horror movie. The needle was over a foot long and wider than a pencil, the doctors and nurses held me down as they speared my arm with it . . . and I screamed as a gushing fountain of blood sprayed into the air and over their crazed, laughing faces. Yaaaaaaggghhhhhh!!!!

THE FEAR

When you think about it, aichmophobia (pronounced: ayk-), or the fear of needles, is a pretty logical and reasonable fear to have. It's basically a fear of being stabbed by a stranger with a sharp, pointy object. And who in his right mind wants that?

Then you have dentists, who wield not only needles, but also drills, pliers, and a whole host of shiny, glinting instruments of torture. There you lie, with your mouth propped open in silent (or at best, grunting) protest, while the dentist sets about scraping, drilling, and pulling at your chompers with wild abandon. Little wonder, then, that odontophobia (the fear of dentists) comes in ahead of needles in the list of common fears.

And finally, you have doctors and nurses—the objects of iatrophobia, or the fear of doctors. They peer and poke at your ears, eyes, and throat, seeming to find all the sorest spots in the course of examining you. Worse yet, they can send you to the hospital, where surgeons might slice you open on the operating table, chop out your tonsils, and goodness knows what else.

What if you woke up in the middle of it all? What if the surgeon was out to get you? What if all doctors, nurses, and dentists were a bunch of lunatics—evil maniacs using their needles, drills, and scalpels as weapons? It's enough to make you feel ill, if you aren't already!

THE REALITY

All right—stop that. Needle injections really aren't that bad, and doctors and dentists aren't out to get you. While some needle, doctor, and dentist phobias begin with one bad experience (like a particularly nasty tooth extraction, or being hastily prodded by a gruff and impatient* doctor), most do not. Most come from those all-powerful scary stories we get from news reports, movies, and other people. Our friends exaggerate stories about injections** and trips to the hospital to make them sound more impressive, dramatic, and interesting. And where there have been one or two doctors over the years who have hurt or killed people, news stories have been focused only on these rare "bad apples," and not on the thousands of good, caring doctors and nurses out there.

---

* And after all, what good is a doctor without patience? Geddit? Doctor . . . patients? Oh, forget it.
** As an example of this—the injection story at the beginning is mine. Although the actual needle turned out to be tiny (and didn't hurt at all), when all my friends heard the story, it was more like the bloodbath detailed here. I probably created a few aichmophobes with that story.

To make things even worse, if you are anxious about visiting a doctor or dentist, your fears can also build and amplify while you wait for your appointment to come.

Ever sit in a doctor's or dentist's waiting room sweating, fidgeting, and generally dreading what might happen when you finally get in there? If so, then you already know that fear doesn't always hit you all at once. It can come as a sudden shock to your system, or it can build and swell inside you, turning from dread to panic, little by little. Which one is worse? Well, that depends on who you ask.

Some people say they hate shocks and surprises, so being pounced upon and eaten by a snarling tiger that appears from nowhere is just about the scariest thing they can think of. But now imagine that you knew that in two days' time, at exactly 10 a.m., you would be attacked and eaten by a snarling tiger, and there was nothing you could do to avoid it.* Would that make you feel better, or worse? Some people might say "better," since knowing about the tiger would help you to prepare for the shock. But would it really help? And how could you prepare for what you know will be a terrifying experience—one that you can't possibly avoid?

For many (if not most) people, knowing about the tiger wouldn't help at all. Right after you were told about it, you'd picture the scene, and begin to worry. At first, this worry (or anxiety) wouldn't look like much

from the outside—maybe a wrinkled brow, tense neck or shoulders, and slightly quickened breathing. Then, as the hours passed, the anxiety would turn into stress, as your brain would react to your tense muscles and fast breathing by assuming you were in trouble and might soon need to run or fight. To help you do this, your brain would then trigger the release of chemicals called hormones into your bloodstream, where they quicken the heart rate and direct blood away from your digestive system and toward your muscles. This would make your muscles even more tense, your breathing even quicker and shallower, and your stomach queasy and nauseous.

Right about now, you would start noticing these signs yourself, and you'd decide that if all this is happening, you must be really scared. Then you'd get more and more anxious and panicked as your body seemed to spiral out of control. Eventually, this cycle of think-react-think-react might build into even bigger physical changes and reactions, like trembling, sobbing, and crying. This is how fear builds up in cycles and stages, from "slightly worried" to "totally losing it."

No one wants to be eaten by a snarling tiger. It would be terrifying. Dreadful. But knowing about it in advance would only give you more time to feel all this terror and dread before it happened.

A similar thing can happen when waiting for anything you believe will be

---

* Even clunking about in a full suit of armor, or locking yourself in a tiger-proof cage all day.

scary or unpleasant, including getting an injection from a doctor, having a tooth pulled by a dentist, or your tonsils removed at the hospital. The difference is that none of these things (trust me) are anywhere near as bad as being eaten by a tiger. In fact, most injections, tooth pulls, and operations are quite painless, and nothing to worry about.

Injections, for example, are usually done with pretty tiny needles—just a few centimeters long and less than a millimeter wide. The reason why some shots (like the BCG shots you get as a teenager to protect against tuberculosis) leave scars is because of a reaction between your skin and the vaccine, not because the needle is scarily massive!

What about dentists? Well, during the course of a visit they may scrape, drill, fill, remove, or fit braces to your teeth. But with a good dentist and a good anesthetic, you probably won't feel much except a bit of pressure against your head.

Doctors, meanwhile, may use their fingers to prod at sore spots (to check for inflammation and internal damage), and may use instruments like a stethoscope (the cold, heart-listening thing), otoscope (the thing they peer into your ear with), or ophthalmoscope (the eye-examining gadget). But none of these instruments or tests really hurts. Afterward, you'll probably be given some medicine and sent home, but even if you are sent to the hospital for surgery, most operations don't hurt either. The anesthesiologist will numb the body area or put you to sleep while the surgeon works,

and you'll wake up the next day missing your tonsils (or appendix, or whatever), but otherwise feeling just a bit sore.

Most of the fear involved in medical phobias comes from not knowing (or being misled about) what really happens when you "get in there." Once you know what to expect, you can control your anxiety and stop it before it builds up into real stress, fear, and panic. What's more, most nurses, doctors, and dentists will even help you to do this by telling you what to expect, and reassuring you about it all as you go along.

THE CHANCES

The odds against a standard injection, examination, or dental operation going wrong and causing you permanent harm are millions to one. As for hospital operations, they may have different risks depending on what needs to be done (tonsil and appendix removals are very common and safe, while kidney and liver transplants are more risky).

But look at it this way—the odds of becoming seriously ill because you avoided an injection, examination, or operation are far, far higher. Nurses, doctors, and dentists are there to heal you, not harm you. So you're better off seeing them whenever you need to, and letting them do their jobs.

THE LOWDOWN

Vaccinations, blood tests, and other needle jabs are nothing to be afraid of. The needles are too small to do any real damage, and most feel more like a "pinch" than a "stab." So no matter what tall tales your friends might tell you about them, there's really no need to panic about getting a jab. If nothing else, a quick pinprick is far less painful and dangerous than catching the actual disease the jab is trying to prevent, as

we'll see in the next section . . .

Doctors and dentists are nothing to be afraid of either. They're there to help, so you should trust them and talk to them rather than live in fear of them. Doctors may have to prod and poke you a bit to properly diagnose what's wrong with you, but they certainly won't hurt you on purpose. In fact, doctors are trained to be sensitive to your pain and your worries, so if you're uncomfortable or afraid, just tell them, and they'll help you through it.

Dentists, too, are trained to be sensitive and to avoid causing you unnecessary pain. Most dentists are so good at this that they can drill and remove teeth without you even feeling a thing. Instead of drilling and scraping, they may use special air abrasion tools—which blast the tooth with a mixture of air and powder at high pressure—or even use lasers to do painless dental work. Most dentists can also give painless injections, by using tiny jabs above the gum line (where you can hardly feel them) to numb an area. And if you do need a bigger injection, they'll often do a couple of these smaller ones first, so that you don't feel the "big one." If you're really afraid of needles and injections, the dentist may even use anesthetic gels or patches instead.

So if your dentist is hurting you, he or she shouldn't be—find a new one! Trust me, there are loads of nice doctors and dentists out there. You just have to give them a chance, and be a little patient.* Now say "ahhhh. . ."

---

* Or a big patient, if you're taller. Heh-heh-heh. Oh, wait—I've already done that joke . . .

Everybody has wisdom teeth—the pairs of molar teeth that sit right at the back of your upper and lower jaws. But some people go their whole lives without them ever poking their way through the surface of the gums, while in others they barge through and press so painfully against your cheeks and other teeth that they have to be removed right away. And being the largest of all the molar teeth, they often don't come out without a fight.

When I was about sixteen years old, the pair of wisdom teeth in my lower jaw decided to make an appearance. First the left one, then the right. The one on the left wasn't painful at all, but the one on the right was scissoring into my cheek and causing a lot of pain. So off to the dentist I went.

Two hours and several anesthetic injections later, I emerged from the dentist's with my face and tongue numb and my gums throbbing. The tooth had, unusually, cracked in half during the operation, so the dentist had to dig out the rest like he was mining for gold. "Hope I don't have to do that again!" I thought. And since the other one seemed fine, I thought I'd gotten away with it.

But two years later, "Ol' Lefty" decided he wasn't happy and began cutting painfully into my other cheek and barging into my other teeth like an unwelcome party guest. Remembering my last tooth-tunneling experience, I put off going to the dentist for as long as I could. But eventually the pain just became too much to bear, and off I went.

Lying back in the chair, I explained to the dentist (a different one this time) how bad it was with the "last one," and how I really wasn't looking forward to what was coming next. While numbing up my gum with injections, she told me she understood completely, and chatted with me about TV and movies while she continued to prod and probe at the tooth with an assortment of blunt metal instruments.

"Do you want to keep it?" she asked suddenly.

"Keep what?" I said.

"Your tooth," she answered.

"Probably not," I said mournfully. "I think I'm going to want to forget about it once it's done. Just let me know when you're about to start pulling so I can prepare myself, OK?"

"Too late," she said. "It's done." And, incredibly, she waved the tooth in front of my face, clamped between what looked like a pair of nutcrackers!

"Eh?" I said. "What?"

"It's done," the dentist replied, smiling. "Do you want it or not?"

"Errr . . . OK. S'pose so . . ." All that fuss over nothing! I was almost disappointed. Almost . . .

That was the day that I lost a chunky wisdom tooth but gained this chunk of wisdom: don't fear the dentist—just get yourself a nice one!

FLESH-EATING BUGS AND FEVERS

A MOST HORRIBLE WAY TO GO

The Ebola virus is one of more than eighteen types of virus that can cause the horrifying disease hemorrhagic fever. Want to know how horrible? OK . . . but unless you have a very strong stomach, I would skip this part if I were you. . . .

Hemorrhagic fever starts with a sore throat, chest pains, a skin rash, and diarrhea. Then your blood fails to clot, your skin starts to bruise, and your spleen, kidneys, and brain begin to swell up. Next you start bleeding from the eyes, nose, and mouth. Finally, just before you slip into a coma and die, you vomit a thick, black sludge of blood and disintegrated internal organs.

Ouch!

THE FEAR Hemorrhagic (or "bleeding") fevers like Ebola are truly the stuff of horror movies. Liquefied organs, horrible skin sores, explosive bleeding . . . On a long list of things you don't ever want to experience, I would definitely put Ebola right at the top. Then there's the famous flesh-eating MRSA bacterium. Since first making news in the late 1990s with the "Killer Bug Ate My Face" headline, it has popped up in news reports at least once or twice a year. It seems that somebody, somewhere is always getting his or her face eaten off, and it's only a matter of time before the hungry monster bug finds its way to you . . .

THE REALITY

Face-eating bugs and organ-liquefying viruses are perfect horror-movie material, and they make very dramatic stories for news reports, novels, and feature films. But they're actually very rare, and very few people are affected by them each year. Being stories, these books, movies, and reports often exaggerate how nasty the bug is—leading us to think that these diseases are everywhere, that we could catch them at any time, and that when we do . . . we're in for an inescapable grisly end.

But in the real world, Ebola has never been seen anywhere outside of a few villages in West Africa, and certainly not anywhere in the developed world, where people seem so terrified of it. In the last twenty years, only three people in the United Kingdom, the United States, and Russia—all laboratory workers—have been infected, and all after accidental jabs with needles. And two of those survived.

Even in the countries where Ebola outbreaks have happened—such as Uganda, Gabon, and the Republic of Congo—it only causes between 10 and 200 deaths per year. That may sound like a lot, but it's nothing compared to the millions who die each year of diseases like tuberculosis and malaria.

Part of the reason for this is that most forms of Ebola aren't very contagious, so they don't spread as easily as the movies and news reports would have you believe. And grisly as it sounds, the really contagious forms of Ebola kill people so quickly that no one has time to leave and seek help, so the virus rarely spreads far beyond the village where an outbreak begins.

As for the "new, infectious, flesh-eating bacteria," they're neither new nor infectious nor actually flesh-eaters at all! The bacterium that causes the "flesh-eating" disease (otherwise known as necrotizing fasciitis) is a rather common one called *staphylococcus aureus* (or SA). It lives on your skin and in your nose, and the worst it usually does is cause (quite harmless) skin or throat infections, which are easily cleared up with a course of antibiotics. The problem comes when the strain of SA you catch becomes resistant to methicillin and other antibiotics normally used to treat these infections. Then it becomes what's known as methicillin-resistant staphylococcus aureus, or MRSA. This is the so-called flesh-eating bug.

But MRSA doesn't actually "eat flesh;" it just releases toxins as the infection develops, which sometimes break down the skin and soft tissues around the infection. When this happens, what starts with a pimple can—if left untreated—turn into a blister or a hole. In a few rare cases, it can lead to more serious (and deadly) infections of the lungs, heart, and brain. But it doesn't actually eat your flesh. And more often than not, the simple, pimplelike infection clears up on its own and leaves you totally unharmed.

THE CHANCES

Outside West Africa, the chances of catching a deadly form of the Ebola virus are next to zero, and even in Africa, your chances of catching it are pretty slim. As for the "flesh-eating" MRSA bug, it affects elderly people far more than it does others. (This is partly because they have weaker immune systems, and partly because they tend to be in hospitals more often, so they have more opportunities to catch it.) But still, even for people over 85, the chances of catching a deadly MRSA strain are about 1 in 1,000, which is still pretty low. For everyone else, the chances are about 1 in 1 million, or small enough to ignore completely.

THE LOWDOWN

As with many of the other health scares we hear so much about, being bombarded with scary stories about killer bugs and viruses gives us the impression that they're both more common and more dangerous than they really are. Ebola and MRSA are dangerous, as they both can cause deadly diseases. But nasty as they are, they're still very rare and are nowhere near as infectious or powerful as the news reports and movies make them out to be.

In the disaster movie *Outbreak*, Ebola spreads around an entire country in days, traveling through the air and infecting whole cities full of people at once. In reality, the Ebola virus can't survive for long in the air, and even if it did cause a countrywide outbreak, it would probably mutate very quickly into a less dangerous form before it had a chance to do that much damage.

In news reports about MRSA, reporters often say the bug is "resistant to all antibiotics" and "can't be treated," when in reality most MRSA infections can still be treated and cured with the antibiotic vancomycin, and other treatments are being developed as we speak.

So don't believe everything you see on TV, in newspapers, or on the Internet. Killer bugs aren't about to attack you, and your face will most likely stay uneaten for life.

FEAR FACTS:

Ebola is in the family of viruses known as filoviruses. "Filo" means "thread" in Latin, and they get this name because, close up, each viral particle looks like a little loop of string. Stringy "filo" pastry gets its name for the same reason . . . but is obviously far safer to eat than Ebola.

Ebola is related to the rabies virus, which is technically more deadly—since rabies kills 100% of those it infects, while Ebola kills "only" 90%.

Another name for Ebola is green monkey fever.

IN THE L

EVENT

WEIGHING THE ODDS

When trying to understand your fears, it's usually not good to think about that one thing you're afraid of and nothing else. In fact, that's a sure way to make it seem bigger and scarier than ever. Instead it helps, if you can, to try to look at scary things in a different way—to see them in the "big picture" of nasty possibilities so that you can understand them in perspective.

Of course, we've already been doing this for every fear we've looked at so far. Every time we look at "The chances" of a scary thing happening and try to put a number on it, we are, in a way, ranking or scoring

it against all the other scary things in the book. But so far, most of the fearsome things we've looked at have had pretty low odds of occurring. Shark attacks, asteroid strikes, and death-by-face-eating-bugs all have odds against them of thousands—or even millions—to one. Most of us look at numbers like these and think something like this: "A million to one? That means it's never going to happen."*That, in a way, is fair enough. But as the numbers get smaller—1 in 10,000, 1 in 1,000, 1 in 100—

* Unless we happen to be playing the lottery, when we think, "That one in a million could be me!"
Funny how the mind works, ain't it?

The answer is actually (c). It doesn't seem right, does it? But it's true. Five heads in a row has the exact same probability of happening as four heads followed by a tail. Or five tails in a row, for that matter. Every time you flip the coin, there's a 1 in 2 (or 50%) chance of it coming up heads, and an equal 50% chance of it coming up tails. And it doesn't matter how many times you flip the coin; those odds never change. Over 1,000 tosses of the coin, the results will tend to balance themselves out, giving somewhere near (but not exactly) 500 heads and 500 tails. But over just five tosses of the coin, getting five heads (or five tails) is actually quite likely, and you or I shouldn't be surprised when it happens.

But we are surprised, because our brains didn't evolve to weigh probabilities, and our intuitions—or gut feelings—tell us that "five heads in a row" must mean "he's got a trick coin with two heads on it or something."*

OK, now let's try something else. When you're looking at the numbers involved in plane crashes, you might come across a pair of facts like this:

- The chances of dying in an airplane crash are about 1 in 4 million.
- Each day, worldwide, around 4 million people travel by airplane.

Looking at these numbers, you might immediately think: "hang on a minute—that means somebody somewhere dies in a plane crash every day!"

our minds tend to start "ramping up" the chances, until we feel like the odds of something happening are much higher than the numbers are actually telling us. This is because the human brain isn't very good at weighing probabilities and chances.

Don't believe me? OK, let me give you a little test.

Let's say I have a coin. The odds of it coming up heads or tails when I flip it should be the same: since there are only two possible outcomes, the chances must be 1 in 2 for each outcome. Right?

OK, now let's say I flip it four times. The first time, it comes up heads. The second time, heads. Third time . . . heads. And the fourth time . . . heads again. Now, which outcome do you think is more likely on the next throw? Is it (a) tails, (b) heads again, or (c) dunno, seems like they're equally likely to me.

If you're like most people, you answered (a). After all, it's come up heads four times already, hasn't it? Five heads in a row has got to be less likely than four heads and a tail.

* Which could also be true. So avoid betting money on coin flips with anyone who does magic tricks as a hobby.

98

But that's simply not true. Fatal plane crashes (as we'll see) are actually very rare. It's just that your head is messing with you again. Like the odds of the flipped coin turning up tails, every time you fly the odds of crashing are roughly the same. For the coin, the odds are 1 in 2; for the plane, the odds are 1 in 4 million. So while it seems like taking that one flight puts you at real risk of being that "1 in 4 million passengers who won't make it off the plane," this simply isn't the case. In reality, the average person would have to take a flight every day for thousands of years before he or she could expect to be in a crash.

Knowing all this, of course, doesn't simply kick the brain into understanding, or remove all your fears in a puff of brainy logic. As we've seen, the brain doesn't quite work that way when it comes to fears. No matter how smart and well-armed with facts and numbers you are, the emotional part of the brain can still kick in and drown out all your lovely logic and probabilities with a single sweep of powerful body responses (tense muscles, sweaty palms, racing pulse) that make us scared all by themselves. So to get around your fears, facts and numbers alone aren't enough. You still have to work on understanding your own emotions and feelings.

Still, getting things in perspective is a good way to start. Especially with scary things—like plane crashes—which seem very likely, but really aren't. On the flip side, it also helps us realize how things that seem perfectly safe, like crossing the road, can actually be more dangerous than flying.

Now, I bet that's got you really worried . . .

PLANES AND FLYING

SMASHED ON THE RUNWAY

In March 1977, the worst airline accident in history happened on the Spanish island of Tenerife. Two jumbo jets collided on a foggy runway, killing 583 people in the double wreck.

As the American plane taxied down the runway, the departing KLM (Dutch) plane suddenly appeared out of the fog. The aircraft was accelerating down the runway at a speed of more than 125 mph. Both pilots tried to accomplish the impossible: the American pilot turned his airliner sharply to the left at full thrust in an attempt to get off the runway, and the Dutch captain forced his plane off the ground in an attempt to fly over the American aircraft—but it was too late . . . The two planes collided, and soon the runway was covered in debris, all of it on fire. Nine hours would pass before the inferno was finally brought under control.

THE FEAR

Pteromerhanophobia,* or the fear of flying, is extremely common. If you don't have it yourself, you almost certainly know someone among your family or friends who does. (I can count six pteromerhanophobes among my lot!) Studies have shown that over half of all children and adults are frightened or anxious at least sometimes when they fly. And it's fairly easy to understand why.

There you are, hurtling through the air in a huge metal tube weighing hundreds of tons over which you have no control. You know it's supposed to be safe, but the more you think about it, the more it seems that this thing really has no business being in the air at all. All that's between you and the treacherous pull of gravity that could bring you crashing back to earth are a few rumbling engines and about 30,000 feet of thin air. You start to sweat as you stare out of the windows. "If that wing cracks," you think to yourself, "we're doomed. Or if just one of those engines cuts out, we'll be plummeting from the sky into a fiery wreck on land, or plunged into the cold, dark ocean, trapped in a mass of twisted metal . . ."

THE REALITY

You've heard it before, you'll hear it again, and you still may never really believe it . . . but plane crashes really are extremely rare events. Especially when you consider how many flights take off and land safely worldwide every day.

Over 4 million people a day travel by plane, which adds up to over 1.7 billion passengers on over 25 million flights per year. Of these, there are only a handful of crashes each year—in some years, none at all. And although airlines based in North America and western Europe account for over two-thirds of all the planes in the sky, less than a quarter of crashes happen on these flights. Typically there is only one crash per year, and often there are no crashes at all. What's more, most accidents happen to poorly maintained planes in developing countries, and we probably wouldn't even hear about them if they didn't make such dramatic pictures and stories for world news reports. So once again, "scary stories" are partly to blame for our fears. Being bombarded with these stories makes us think plane crashes are more common and more of a danger to us than they really are.

*   And if you think that's a long word, then check this one out: hippopotomonstrosesquippedaliophobia. Believe it or not, that's the name for the fear of long words. After reading that monster, I think I might have it too . . .

In fact, thanks to improvements in aircraft design, pilot training, and air traffic control technology, flying has become safer than ever over the last few decades. While the total number of flights each year has been steadily increasing, the number of fatal crashes has stayed roughly the same—which, if you think about it, means that an increasing number of flights are arriving safely each year. More planes, more flights, but fewer crashes per flight.* Which is nice to know.

THE CHANCES

The chances of your particular flight ending in a fatal crash depend a little on what kind of plane you're flying in, and which airline you fly with. Believe it or not, large planes like jumbo jets have better safety records than small propeller planes that seat far fewer people—partly because they're more stable in flight, and partly because they're checked so thoroughly before they're allowed to take off. Among the airlines, some have perfect safety records, without a single fatal crash in millions of flights, while other airlines have a number of crashes to their name.

That said, even the "worst" of these (like Cubana Airlines and Air Zimbabwe)

have an average of only one crash in every 18,000 flights. Most airlines have "crash rates" of between 1 in 2.5 million and 1 in 5 million. In all, the chances of any one person being in a fatal plane crash average out at around 1 in 4 million—about 50 times less likely than being struck by lightning, and about 8 times less likely than being killed by an asteroid impact.** How's that for weighing the odds?

BE PREPARED!

* That's the total number of flights divided by the total number of crashes each year, NOT the number of times each plane crashes on a single flight. You wouldn't catch me on a plane if we had to calculate that!
** Which, by my calculations, puts the odds of your plane crashing after being struck by an asteroid and a lightning bolt at the same time at roughly 1 in 160,000,000,000,000,000 (160 quadrillion)—just in case you were wondering.

THE LOWDOWN

The numbers tell us that flying really is nothing to be afraid of, yet fear of flying is incredibly common. This is partly because our brains don't listen to numbers alone, and partly because many people who think they're afraid of flying are actually afraid of something associated with flying.

Our brains haven't had a chance to evolve a fear of "flying in planes," as they haven't really evolved much at all in the time that we've had airplanes (which is only about 100 years, after all). What our brains and bodies can (and do) react to is being squashed into a tight space with thin air; seeing the ground sprawling out hundreds or thousands of feet below; accelerating suddenly to speeds of over 300 mph; feeling trapped and unable to stop, get off, and escape; flying over a wide expanse of water; being in a wide, dark, and unknowable sky, and so on. You can probably see how lots of small fears like these can easily add up to a big fear of the whole flight experience.

So getting over your fear of flying (if you have one) isn't really about understanding airplanes and flight procedures. It's about understanding what it is that's really making you uncomfortable, and working on your emotional response to that.

In the meantime, you can rest (or at the very least, sit) safe in the knowledge that flying really is the safest way to travel. And you can make sure you stay extra safe and secure by doing the following every time you fly, just in case something should happen:

- Keep your seat belt fastened whenever you're in your seat. But don't worry—this is less to do with preparing for a crash than it is avoiding getting bumped and bruised during unexpected air "chop" or "turbulence."
- Make sure you study the plane safety card so you know how to get out if you need to. Crashes and emergency landings are extremely rare, but if they do happen, you need to know how to get out quickly in case there's a fire, or the plane has to land on water.
- Listen to everything the flight attendants tell you, every time you fly, no matter how many times you think you've heard it. They're there to keep you and the other passengers safe, so if you ignore them, you're putting yourself and others at risk. Help them to do their job by listening and following instructions, and you'll be like an extra member of the safety crew!
- Once you're prepared like this, you can feel happier and more in control. Then you can sit back, relax, and enjoy the whoosh and rumble of takeoff, the in-flight movies and games, the peculiar airline snacks, and the whole flying experience.

COWBOY PILOT "COMFORTS" FRIGHTENED PASSENGERS

Since I now have family in both the U.K. and the United States, I spend a lot of time flying back and forth across the Atlantic Ocean to see them. I don't mind flying so much, and I actually kind of enjoy the takeoff and landing, when the plane goes whooshing down the runway. But few people, I think, really enjoy it when the plane shakes and pitches around—a result of uneven airflow over the wings, known as chop or (if it's stronger) turbulence. Few people, it seems, except the pilot of one particular flight from Texas to London, which I "experienced" a few years ago.

Not long after takeoff, turbulence began to rock the cabin, and the seat belt signs pinged on as the passengers jostled around in their seats. Having flown many times before, I knew that the "ping!" noise was usually followed by another "ping!" noise as the loudspeaker came on, followed by a comforting announcement from the captain or a flight attendant. Something like: "Ladies and gentlemen, please return to your seats. As you can see, the 'fasten seat belt' signs have been activated, so please ensure your seat belts are properly secured, and return all tray tables to an upright position. Just a little bit of choppy air, and we should be through it before too long. Nothing to worry about."

Instead, this time, there was a "ping!" but no announcement, just breathing. Everyone looked up as the plane continued to pitch around. Eventually a message from the captain began.

"Ladies and gentlemen . . ." and then nothing.

Suddenly, the plane seemed to drop straight down out of the sky for a full two seconds, and almost everyone on the plane (me included) made an automatic, fearful, high-pitched "Uunnnhhhhhhhhhh!" sound.

"Woaaah!" cheered the captain over the loudspeaker, sounding like a cowboy on a bucking horse.

The plane dropped again. For three seconds this time. A very long three seconds.

"Unnnnnnnnnnnnnnnhhhhh!" went the passengers.

"Ha-haaaaa!!" chortled the captain, clearly insane.

Then the shaking and pitching seemed to soften, and eventually it stopped altogether.

Were we safe? Was it over? All the passengers looked at each other with nervous smiles, awaiting an announcement from the captain to tell us what was going on.

"Ping!"

We all froze, listening.

"Ladies and gentlemen . . ." began the captain.

"Yes?" we all thought. "What?"

". . . you'd have to pay good money for a ride like that at Disneyland."

The whole plane erupted in a ripple of groaning, nervous laughter. The sound was a mixture of giggling at the awful joke and pure relief that it was all, apparently, over.

I've flown many times since, but I've never experienced turbulence quite that bad again. Nor have I laughed quite as heartily as I did that day, thanks to the cowboy captain.

RUNAWAY TRAINS

DISASTROUS DERAILMENT

At 10:56 a.m. on June 3, 1998, a German InterCity Express (ICE) train was traveling at 125 mph when it derailed and slammed into the pillars of a road bridge crossing over the tracks. The concrete bridge came crashing down on the train wreck and the many passengers inside. After the crash, rescue workers toiled for hours, sifting through twisted metal and amputated body parts in an effort to find survivors. In all, 101 people died and most of the 100 survivors were seriously injured. It was the worst train accident in Europe since 1945.

THE FEAR Ever stand on a platform as a big train whips through without stopping? That gives you some idea of the terrifying momentum that a speeding train has. A 100-ton train weighs over 50 times as much as the average car. So in terms of momentum (mass multiplied by speed), being hit by a train traveling 125 mph is like being hit by a car traveling over 6,000 mph.*

Now imagine being inside a train like this as it hurtles out of control and derails. The terrifying screech of metal as your carriage folds up like an accordion and tumbles from the tracks. The sickening lurch as it rolls onto its side or roof, and the whole structure caves in . . .

THE REALITY

The fear of trains (or siderodromophobia) isn't nearly as common as that of airplanes or boats. But it certainly does crop up, most often with people who have been in a real train accident at some earlier point in their lives. However, it can also strike people who have no train-related upsets in their past at all, like those who were passengers in road (rather than rail) accidents. And this gives us a clue that something else might be happening with train-o-phobes.

Just as with the fear of airplanes, the fear of trains can have little to do with trains themselves. It may instead be a general fear of speed (tachophobia), of movement or motion (kinetophobia), or of being locked in (cleithrophobia). After all, all these things are part of the train rider's experience. Trains move very fast, jerk to a start or halt, and wobble from side to side as they run. And many have doors that lock after departure.

Those things aside, riding a train is, in itself, definitely nothing to be afraid of. Traveling by rail is safer than traveling by air or sea, and it's far, far safer than traveling by road. The risk of being injured when traveling by train is at least twenty times less than when traveling by car.

In fact, the total number of train passengers killed on U.S. railways since they were introduced in the 1800s is far less than the number of car passengers killed on U.S. roads in a single year. And trains in Europe and Japan are statistically even safer.

---

* No car has ever done anywhere near 6,000 mph, of course. The fastest jet planes can't even do half that speed. And the fastest car yet has managed only 750 mph. But you get the idea.

THE CHANCES

The chances of being in a train crash vary across the globe, as more fatal crashes happen in developing countries than in developed countries. But train safety is generally improving worldwide every year, and the odds of being caught in a fatal crash are still extremely low—between 1 in 60,000 and 1 in 140,000.

THE LOWDOWN

Trains are actually the safest way to travel quickly overland (or underground), and generally only a danger to us when we're in front of them rather than on them. While train passenger deaths are rare in the U.S., every year over 300 people die after falling in front of trains, messing around on train tracks, or stopping their cars at railroad crossings. So the lesson here is clear: getting on a train won't kill you, but getting on a train track will.

As with plane crashes and other rare transportation accidents, train wrecks make for dramatic news. So when one happens somewhere in the world, it's usually all over the TV within the hour. Car accidents, on the other hand, are so common that they scarcely ever make the news (unless perhaps somebody famous is involved). Seeing this over and over again tricks us into thinking that train crashes are common and car crashes are rare, when the truth is quite the opposite.

In fact, if all the drivers in North America and Europe who travel to work in cars every day switched to traveling by train (that's assuming they could, of course), it would save over 50,000 lives every year, or over 150 lives each day. How's that for a train of thought?

FEAR FACTS:

Because they're so heavy and fast, moving trains have enormous amounts of momentum and are very difficult to slow down quickly. When the driver on an average passenger train traveling at 55 mph hits the brakes, it travels over a mile before stopping.

The fastest trains in the world are Magnetic Levitation (MagLev) trains, which use electrically powered magnets to hover (or levitate) above their tracks. With no friction between the wheels and tracks to slow them down, MagLev trains have been clocked at over 360 mph, otherwise known as "pant-wetting speed"!

SHIPS, BOATS, AND THE SEA

TRAGEDY STRIKES AT SEA

"*Mayday, Mayday. This is Estonia...*" *read the message, recorded by marine rescue authorities on the Finnish coast. The message broke off abruptly, suggesting a loss of power—perhaps water entering the machine room. It was the first and last contact with the ship. On board, severe vibrations woke passengers in their cabins. Many were unable to leave their rooms before all the lights went out. Eyewitnesses talked of panic and of people being left behind in the crush. . . . There was little time to escape. Within a matter of minutes—not more than 30, according to some accounts—the ship had capsized and sunk, with the loss of more than 800 lives.*

THE FEAR Most of us have heard of the sinking of the *Titanic*, but that was almost a century ago, and there have been many other tragic accidents at sea in the years between. Like the *Herald of Free Enterprise*, a car-and-passenger ferry traveling from Belgium to England, which capsized just 2 miles out of port, drowning 193 people inside in March 1987. Or the *Estonia*, another ferry, which capsized en route from Estonia to Sweden, in which 852 people lost their lives in the icy waters of the Baltic Sea in September 1994. Or the *Princess of Stars*, capsized by a typhoon in the Philippines in June 2008, drowning over 800 passengers on board. All of these tragedies remind us of just how vulnerable we are when floating on the cruel, merciless ocean, and they all feed into thalassophobia—the fear of the sea.

THE REALITY

It's true that whenever we put out to sea, we are vulnerable to the wind and waves. No ship is completely storm proof, and even the largest cargo ships and oil tankers can be capsized or sunk by the worst kinds of weather. In fact, ships of this size (over 6,000 tons) are the riskiest to be on—you're roughly twice as likely to suffer drowning or serious injury on board one of these compared with smaller vessels. That's the bad news.

The good news is that boats designed to carry people (rather than cargo) are much safer, and passenger ferries are the safest ships of all. Ferries very, very rarely sink. The tragic losses of the *Estonia* and the *Herald of Free Enterprise* were not caused by a leaky hull or a faulty pump. They were the result of human mistakes. In both cases, people on board made mistakes that put the whole vessel at risk. The same was true of the *Titanic*. It wasn't really the monster iceberg that sank that ship; it was the captain.*

We've learned a lot from these past disasters, and used that knowledge to make ferries and other ships much safer. As a result, there have been no ferry passenger deaths in European waters since the *Estonia* disaster back in 1994. In the United States, over 200 million passengers use ferry systems every year, yet there were virtually no fatalities between the *General Slocum* ferry incident of 1904 and the Staten Island Ferry crash of 2003. In North America and Europe, ferries are by far the safest form of travel. And while there have been more frequent incidents elsewhere in the world, ferries still rate as a pretty safe way to travel when compared to smaller vessels like yachts and speedboats.

* . . . who decided to run the *Titanic* at top speed, in the dark, in an area known to have icebergs. Not so smart, perhaps.

As for these, there are a good number of small motorboat accidents each year, but very few are the result of faulty boats or boat equipment. Boating accidents are almost always caused by drivers or pilots who aren't paying attention, are driving carelessly, or are driving too fast. And of all the fatal accidents each year, an incredible 80–90% happen to people not wearing life jackets. So the lesson is clear—boats are quite safe, as long as you handle them responsibly and wear the proper gear.

THE CHANCES

The odds of being in a fatal boating accident depend on how often you go boating, how experienced you are, and how you act while on board. When wearing a life jacket while boating on a lake or close to shore, the odds of a fatal accident are very low. Speeding out to sea wearing nothing but a T-shirt . . . much higher. As for ferries, the odds differ depending on where you are in the world and what safety standards are like there, but in general ferry travel is very safe. In all, the odds of dying in a water transportation accident are between 1 in 7,000 (for drowning) and 1 in 20,000 (for other kinds of onboard accidents).

THE LOWDOWN

There will always be some risk involved in putting out to sea, as we can never perfectly predict the weather and sea conditions that often lead to accidents. But since most boating accidents are caused by people driving recklessly, colliding with other boats, or falling overboard without life jackets, it's largely up to us how safe we stay when boating. As for ferries and larger ships, if you're on one of those, you're about as safe as you can get while at sea. And if wind and wave conditions get too "choppy," the captain will most likely not put out to sea anyway. (Planes and trains generally won't leave airports or stations if bad weather makes the skies or rails too hazardous either. Ship, plane, and train operators work by strict rules governing when they are and aren't allowed to set off in bad weather. So have some trust in them too!)

As with the fear of planes and trains, the fear of being at sea is often more about the environment than the ship itself. You may have a more general fear of water or drowning, of the open space that surrounds you when you're on the open sea, or—if you suffer from seasickness—just the fear of vomiting (emetophobia). Figuring out which of these you suffer from would be the first step in working around a fear of being on board a boat, which usually means trying to get comfortable in shallow lakes or swimming pools first.

If you can't swim, learning to swim (or even to scuba dive)* with a patient instructor can be a great way to get more comfortable in the water. From there, you can try boarding boats while they're docked or on land so that you can get used to being around them. Then by the time you take your first sailing trip, you'll feel a lot more in control of your negative feelings—or maybe not even feel them. Most of all, remember to take it at your own speed, and your own pace. Do that, and it's smooth sailing.

---

* Seriously—there's nothing better for curing a fear of the sea than becoming a fish for a day!

CARS

THE LANE CHANGE HE'LL NEVER FORGET

"I looked over my shoulder to see the other driver suddenly brake and swerve. From that moment it seemed as though everything was in slow motion. His car hit the rear of mine, sending me into a 180-degree spin. My car struck the metal barrier dividing the highway, flipped over it, bounced upside down, and rolled once more before coming to rest in the fast lane on the opposite side of the road. The sunroof had collapsed onto the back of my head, and I was bleeding heavily—struggling to retain consciousness.

"By some miracle, an army convoy had been traveling in the opposite direction and managed to stop all oncoming traffic before my vehicle was hit again. They stayed with me until the helicopter arrived and airlifted me to the hospital."

—Paul D., U.K.

THE FEAR Unlike most of the scary things we've looked at so far, car crashes are not rare events. They're extremely common, and unlike those you see in movies and TV series, people rarely walk away from a real car crash completely uninjured. When two cars collide head-on at 30 mph, the effect is much the same as one car hitting a brick wall at 60 mph. Your head snaps forward and back with a vicious whipping motion, causing injury to the brain, neck, and spine. Your arms and legs can be smashed and crushed within the car's crumpling metal frame. And even if contact with a seat belt or steering wheel stops you from flying through the windshield, your heart can continue moving forward even after your chest is stopped, crushing it against your breastbone. At least 50 million people are seriously injured in car crashes every year. No wonder, then, that so many of the victims suffer from amaxophobia (or the fear of riding in a car) for years afterward.

THE REALITY

The simple truth is, on a list of "safe ways to get around," cars are almost at the bottom.* This is partly because of the huge number of them on the roads—over 600 million of them at the last count—and because cars are just used more than other forms of transportation. With that many cars swarming together on the world's roads, you would perhaps expect a good number of accidents and collisions.

But while the growing number of cars makes crashes more likely, the good news is that cars themselves are becoming safer to drive. Newer car models have sensors that can alert the driver if he drifts between lanes on a highway, and brakes that can slow the car without skidding in an emergency. If a crash does happen, specially designed "crumple" zones within the car's metal body scrunch up to absorb impact from the outside. Meanwhile, inside the car, rapidly inflating airbags cushion the passengers from being bashed against hard surfaces. And perhaps most important of all, seat belts prevent the driver and passengers from being thrown against (or through) the windshield.

Thanks to safety features like these, many crash victims' lives are saved at speeds under 50 mph. Most crashes that result in deaths happen at speeds over 50 mph, or where the passengers aren't wearing seat belts (especially in the backseat). And this brings us to the main thing that affects how safe car travel really is—the driver.

* In fact, only motorcycles are worse. So maybe my mom was on to something when she told me I couldn't have one. Plus I was only 11 when I asked for it . . .

In a few rare cases, the car causes the crash when its brakes, tires, or steering malfunction. But over 95% of crashes are due to drivers—driving too fast, too recklessly, or simply not paying close enough attention to the road and other cars. Poor or dangerous drivers fail to adjust their speed to suit the traffic and weather conditions (like a road made slippery by ice or pelting rain). They also drive too close to other cars, and make sudden turns and risky maneuvers. Although these drivers think they're in control of the car, all of these things leave them unable to react if something goes wrong—like when the car in front suddenly brakes, or their tires slip on the wet road.

Many people who think of themselves as "good" drivers aren't altogether safe either. They can easily be distracted when they fiddle with radios, CD players, phones, food wrappers, and drinks bottles while they drive. Even conversations with other passengers can be dangerously distracting. These drivers think they can do two things at once, but in reality the brain can only focus fully on one task at a time. So paying even a little attention to these "other" things

means they can't pay full attention to the road, and just as with the "reckless" drivers, this leaves them unable to react in an emergency.

To stay safe on the roads we should all try to avoid these dangerous driving habits. For the driver, that means driving responsibly and safely, and not allowing yourself to be distracted. For the passengers, that means making sure you're not distracting the driver too much. So no more fighting over the armrest/games console/last bag of chips, all right?*

THE CHANCES

Car crashes are pretty common, and most people will experience at least one car accident within their lifetimes. The chances of being seriously injured or killed in a crash depend a little on where you live in the world (and how crowded the roads are), and a little on how old the driver is (drivers under 25 and over 75 are most at risk). But mostly it depends on how safe and careful the driver is. The odds range from 1 in 100 (for dangerous drivers on crowded roads) to 1 in 18,000 (for

* I mean it. I'll turn this thing around, and then no one gets to go to Disney World.

safe drivers on near-empty roads). For the average driver or passenger in the United States, Europe, or Australia, the odds are probably around 1 in 1,500. Not terrible, but not too great either.

THE LOWDOWN

Traveling by car is such a common, everyday thing that we almost forget how dangerous it can be. It seems perfectly safe, but with so many cars on the road, there's always the chance of an accident or crash. You're far more likely to be involved in an accident when traveling by car than you are when traveling by boat, train, plane, or bicycle. In fact, over 97% of serious transportation accidents involve cars rather than other methods of travel.

So it makes sense to stay safe when traveling by car, just in case. Most of us will never experience a serious, life-threatening car crash. But proper driving behavior can help ensure we never do, and the proper use of car safety features can save our lives if the worst does happen. So whenever and wherever you're hitting the road, always make sure you do the following:

- Sit in the right place, and buckle up. Children 12 and under are generally safer in the backseat, but sitting in the back is NOT SAFER AT ALL IF YOU DON'T USE A SEAT BELT. People often forget or neglect to use seat belts in the back, as the seats in front give them a feeling of security. But in a real crash, you can fly right over the front seats and through the windshield, maybe also injuring or killing the person in front of you.
- Sit up straight in your seat, rather than squirming around and letting the seat belt slip off your shoulder or up over your stomach. Used correctly, a seat belt will decrease your risk of dying in a serious crash by over 61%. Used incorrectly, it won't work as well and could actually injure you.
- Don't dangle your arms or legs out the window while the car is moving. In a serious crash, you might never see those limbs again.
- Don't distract the driver by jumping around, making too much noise, or doing anything to make them turn around in their seat to look at you.
- Take care as you get in or out of parked cars. Look for passing traffic before you open doors, and take special care as you get out of the car, always exiting on the curb side if you can.

FEAR FACTS:
Every year, around 1.2 million people are killed in car accidents, and at least 48 million more are injured worldwide. In the United States, someone dies in a car accident, on average, every 13 minutes.

ROADS

THE REAL KILLERS

Over 1,000 children and young adults are killed on the world's roads every day.

Think about that for a minute—a thousand, every day. That's an entire school full of people gone with every setting sun.

Worldwide, no other thing kills so many young people between the ages of ten and twenty-four. No animal, no disease, no war, and no other type of accident poses a larger threat to the survival of kids, teenagers, and young adults than the common car. If horror movies reflected the real dangers in our lives, then the actors wouldn't be chased by ghosts, monsters, aliens, and crazed murderers—they would be hit at random by murderous cars, driven by ordinary people.

THE FEAR Being struck by a car while on a bicycle or on foot is a genuinely terrifying experience. You could be thrown several yards in the air and land hard on the road with scrapes and broken bones. You could bounce up and over the front of the car that hits you, crashing against the glass windshield and suffering terrible cuts and head injuries. Or worst of all, you could be dragged beneath the wheels of a car, van, or truck as its terrible weight grinds and crushes you beneath.

But interestingly, there is no name for the fear of "being run over," as very few people actually have it. For all the dangers they pose to us, hardly anyone is actually afraid of cars, or of the perilous roads on which they speed past us. It's as if people are ignoring a herd of massive, fast-moving metal monsters that are constantly whipping around us—monsters that can injure or kill anyone unfortunate enough to stray before them. If you think about it, perhaps we *should* be afraid . . .

THE REALITY

OK, so this one really *is* a serious danger. Road-traffic accidents are so common that many of us have been in them, seen them firsthand, or at the very least know somebody who has been in one. And they're never a pretty sight.

Tough as it is, the human body is no match for a speeding car. Even at 40 mph, bones break and skulls shatter easily against the massive momentum generated by two tons of moving steel. Lucky traffic accident victims are bounced clear of the car and escape with minor injuries like broken wrists or ribs. The less lucky ones crack their heads when they fall, bounce into other objects, or slip under the wheels of the vehicle—all of which can prove fatal.

So should you be cowering away from road traffic, or happily strolling and cycling among it? The answer is neither. You should always stay aware of just how dangerous road traffic can be, but if you take care when crossing roads and riding your bike, there's no reason why you can't safely and comfortably share the roads with cars, buses, and trucks.

This is because cars and other vehicles very rarely mount curbs or sidewalks to hit pedestrians, or suddenly swerve in the road to hit cyclists. It's usually the pedestrian or cyclist who causes the accident by entering the path of a car unexpectedly. This often happens for one of three reasons:

1) The car driver doesn't expect you to be in the road. This can happen when you cross the road at a corner or on the brow of a hill, or when you step out from behind a parked car or bus. To the driver, you seem to have appeared out of nowhere, and he hit you before he could even react.

2) The driver doesn't see you in the road. This can happen when you're crossing the road or riding your bike at night, especially if you're wearing dark clothing.

3) The driver sees you but cannot stop in time. This can happen if you cross the road away from pedestrian crossings and traffic islands, in "fast" stretches of road where cars tend to pick up speed. The driver might see you and brake, but the fast-moving car may run or skid into you anyway.

If you can avoid putting yourself in any of these situations, then you're (almost) guaranteed to avoid getting into accidents on the road.

THE CHANCES

The odds of being fatally injured in a traffic accident vary across the world. They depend on how many cars are on the roads, how safe the roads are to cross, and how well car drivers, cyclists, and pedestrians stick to the laws and rules of the road. But in general the odds are fairly low, and a little better for cyclists (about 1 in 4,000) compared with pedestrians (about 1 in 500). Don't get too cocky if you're on a bike, though—there are more pedestrians around than cyclists! Plus many cyclists wear protective helmets, while only the very strangest pedestrians do . . .

THE LOWDOWN

Nobody wants to be hit by a car, but plenty of people are hit, each and every day. Many of these accidents could easily be avoided. Some accidents are caused by reckless or bad drivers, but many (perhaps most) are the result of pedestrians and cyclists who aren't careful when using the roads. "Taking proper care" means you need to:

- Cross the road at a safe place, like a pedestrian (zebra) crossing or traffic island. In particular, never cross at a bend in the road or near the brow of a hill, where approaching cars won't see you in time. Likewise, don't step out (or if on a bike, pull out) from between or behind parked cars or buses—you'll be hidden from view until the last minute, which is just asking for trouble.
- Make sure, wherever you cross, that you stop, look both ways, and listen for traffic before you cross the road. Listening is important because fast-moving cars can appear quickly, even after you've first checked that the coast is clear. For the same reason, remember to keep on looking and listening as you cross.
- If you're on a bike or walking on the side of a road with no pavement, face oncoming traffic and make sure you are easily visible. This means brightly colored clothing during the day, and bright clothing AND lights at night.
- If you ride a bike, wear a helmet. (Who cares if it looks a bit uncool? If you're hit, it could save your life.) And make sure it's properly fitted and fastened.
- Learn the rules of the road, like the Highway Code for both cyclists and pedestrians. You can also take a cycling proficiency test, which will make you a safer and better bike rider.

Finally, remember this—as common as road accidents are, most kids make it through childhood (and most adults through their entire lives) without ever being knocked down or run over.

So treat the roads with the respect they deserve and you can make sure you're in the "road-safe for life" group, rather than in the other, less fortunate one.

THE DAY I HIT A CAR

Growing up, almost every kid I knew rode a bicycle, and I had at least five friends who had been hit by cars while on them. My best friend Darren was hit by a van as he cycled around a traffic circle. He was hit from the side; his leg was impaled on a piece of sharp, twisted metal sticking out of the front bumper; and he was dragged almost 50 feet along the road. Incredibly, he survived with a scar on his leg and little more.

My friend Sarah was in a child's seat on the back of her dad's bike when the two were hit by a truck. The truck tipped over sideways as it swerved to avoid them, and fell onto them as it rolled right over. Her dad was thrown clear, but Sarah was stuck beneath the truck in the twisted, tangled wreckage of the bike. It took three firefighters with cutting gear over an hour to get her out, but she escaped, amazingly, with just a few bumps and bruises and a scar on her hand.

As far as I know, though, I was unique among my friends in being the only one to crash into a car rather than be hit by one.

I was on my bike, thundering down an alleyway that ran behind my house—a steep, downhill corridor between the neighbors' fences and backyards on either side. The end of the steep valley opened out onto the pavement, curb, and road of a cul-de-sac at the bottom. I often raced down this alley on my bike, picking up speed, and jumping off the curb at the bottom to land with a satisfying thunk on the (usually deserted) road.

This time, however, it wasn't deserted. At least not by the time I got to the bottom.

As I steadily picked up speed, the fences whooshing by on either side, I suddenly spotted a car pulling up to the curb at the end of the alleyway. I tried the brakes, but they failed. Oops! Been meaning to fix those. Careering helplessly toward the side of the car, I tried to slow the bike by dragging my feet on the ground, but it was too late. WHAM! My bike stopped as it hit the side door of the car, while I kept going, over the top of it. I crash-landed face-first in the road on the other side, carving wide, gravel-filled grazes into my right cheek and forehead.

The woman driving the car, at first alarmed by the thump and the sight of a wide-eyed kid flying over her roof, started shouting at me for denting her door. Thankfully, a neighbor (also my friend's dad and a local doctor) saw the whole thing, rescued me from angry-car-lady, and spent the next hour patching me up before taking me home.

The graze eventually healed without a scar. But before it did, the single, huge scab running from my jaw to my hairline stuck around for weeks, looking like a giant Triscuit stuck to my face. My brother—always a sensitive soul—called me "Ryvita" right through that month.

Still—as car accidents go, I was luckier than most. It certainly made me more careful on my bike—and around cars—from that day on.

CHAPTER 5

IN THE BAD PLACE

FROM FEARS TO PHOBIAS

What's the difference between a fear and a phobia? Are they totally different, or basically the same thing? And where, exactly, do all these fears and phobias come from?

Well, we've already seen that fears come partly from the ancient history of our species (and the species that we descended from). Just like our eyes, ears, thumbs, lungs, and brains, most of our basic fears evolved because they came in very handy for keeping us safe, and have helped our species to survive.

Eyes and ears, of course, helped our ancestors to hunt, to detect dangerous animals, and to know when a thunderstorm was coming. But it was fear that made them shrink back from the snakes, the lions, and the lightning—fear that kept them alive in the presence of these and other dangers.

Fear is especially important to young animals (including human babies and toddlers), because they're not really capable of looking after themselves. Or rather, they don't yet know enough about the world to keep themselves safe from harm. Very young babies aren't actually afraid of much at all—or at least nowhere near as many things as older children are. Few things make babies cry out in fear (rather than in hunger, or in discomfort at a freshly filled diaper), but the two most common fears are: (1) being left alone, and (2) being handed to a strange, new person they're not familiar with. And if you think about it, that makes sense. A baby doesn't have to be afraid of much—it spends almost all of its time close (or even attached) to its mother, so is generally pretty well-protected. The only thing a baby really has to fear is being abandoned, or being grabbed by someone who isn't one of its parents.

Young children, on the other hand, can toddle further from their parents and have more chances to get themselves into trouble. If young children weren't at least a little bit afraid of the dark, high places, snakes, spiders, and thunderclaps, then they would have a lot less chance of surviving to become teenagers and adults. Fears keep young children wary of the world's dangers while they figure out how everything works. Most things are considered "dangerous, until proven safe." Then, one by one, kids unlearn these fears as they grow up and learn to interact safely with the animals, people, and environment around them.

Phobias, however, are a bit different from fears. Phobias are fears that stretch out longer—or loom bigger in your mind—than they really should. Phobias make you more afraid of things than you should be, and left unchecked they can stop you from living a normal, happy life.

Most phobias are the result of a childhood fear that never went away. Sometimes this happens because the person had a really bad experience when they were little, like being bitten by a dog, or swallowing water and choking in a swimming pool. But more often, a fear becomes a long-lasting phobia because the person has never really had to get over it. Instead, they take steps to avoid the "scary" thing at all costs. And while this does allow them to avoid feeling frightened and anxious, it also makes them more anxious about the "scary" thing every time they do it. So when they finally do encounter a dog, an airplane, a swimming pool, or whatever it is they're afraid of, it seems more terrifying than ever before. The fear response is now way out of proportion to how scary the dog, plane, or pool actually is. This is the main thing that separates fears from phobias.

In our prehistoric past, our ancestors had to hunt the world's forests and grasslands, and fish the world's seas and lakes to survive. But no hunter with a phobia of snakes in the grass would do very well on the hunt. And a fisherman with a phobia of being on the water would be lucky to catch anything at all. So just as fears can help very young children to survive, they can also do harm, by preventing us from doing the things we need to do as adults to live and thrive.

The problem is, unless they grow up in the wilderness or countryside and still have to hunt or gather their own food, many children today can reach adulthood without ever learning to swim, to deal with snakes, or to cope with being alone and exposed in the dark. Most of the world's population now lives in cities and towns, where:

- no one is far from anyone else
- electricity provides light after dark
- people buy their fish, meats, and vegetables, rather than braving the dark seas and forests to fish, hunt, and gather food for themselves
- snakes and other wild animals are very rarely seen.

Little wonder, then, that far more phobias are seen in city dwellers than in those who live off the land.

What do you do, then, if you've already got a phobia? Well, as usual, don't panic! There are ways to get around a phobia if you want to, or at the very least to become more comfortable with the idea of having one. So read on, and let's delve into the deepest, darkest depths of the mind, where fears lurk unseen inside us all . . .

THE DARK

THE THING IN THE CELLAR

"*George did not like the cellar, and he did not like going down the cellar stairs, because he always imagined there was something down there in the dark. . . . He did not even like opening the door to flick on the light, because he always had the idea that while he was feeling for the light switch, some horrible, clawed paw would settle lightly over his wrist . . . and then jerk him down into the darkness that smelled of dirt and wet and dim, rotted vegetables. . . . It was the smell of something for which he had no name . . . creature which would eat anything but which was especially hungry for boy-meat.*"

—From *It*, by Stephen King

THE FEAR
What is it that makes being alone in the dark so terrifying? Simple—you've got no idea what could be lurking in it! Imagine this:

Feeling your way through the lightless depths of a cave, your hands stretched out before you, your fingers suddenly fall upon a mass of writhing worms or scuttling spiders . . .

Camping in a forest on a moonless night, you hear a rustle of leaves and a cracking twig outside your tent. Breathing hard, you poke your head outside to investigate, but you see only pitch blackness . . . and the sounds are getting louder and closer . . .

Waking in your bed in the middle of the night, you suddenly feel a presence in the room. Is it a creeping burglar? A freakish monster? An evil spirit? You're desperate to know, but to switch on the light you'd have to cross the room, to make a noise . . . and then it would know you were there . . .

THE REALITY

Nyctophobia, or fear of the dark, is extremely common in children, and surprisingly common in adults too. Like many phobias, it comes from a fear we're born with—a healthy fear that can help us to avoid danger and harm.

We humans, like most mammals, are very visual creatures. We depend on our eyesight for all kinds of things, like spotting food, recognizing faces, judging distances, catching, throwing, aiming, dodging, fighting, and more.

Robbed of our sense of sight, most of us tend to . . . well, freak out a bit. We find it hard to relax, hard to keep our balance, and hard not to jump at the slightest sound or touch. If you want to test this out, try closing your eyes and slowly walking around the room. You'll probably find that your breathing will get faster, you'll flinch at every object you brush past or bump into, and you'll desperately want to cheat and open your eyes throughout the experiment. Not easy to do calmly, is it?

In one way, this makes perfect sense. No one likes bumping into or tripping over things. So a healthy fear of being cast into darkness will slow you down, make you more alert, and make you move carefully enough to avoid objects and pitfalls. To our ancestors living on the plains and savannahs of Africa, this fear was obviously very important for survival. If they weren't so wary of the dark, then a lot more of them would have ended up accidentally strolling into rivers and ravines, or straight into lions, rhinos, and people from unfriendly tribes. What's more, this instinct still protects us today—even those of us who don't live with wild animals and terrain. If we're outside in a town or city at night, we don't want to wander down dark alleyways or dawdle into dangerous building sites either.

The problem is that this instinctive, "healthy" fear of the dark and real nyctophobia are two different things. It's one thing to be alert in darkened places and quite another thing to have a paralyzing terror of the darkness itself. People with a real phobia of the dark can't sleep without the lights on, panic when the lights go out, and can't enter a darkened room without a thumping heartbeat and a churning stomach. Once a fear turns into a phobia like this, it can stop people from living happy lives, as they feel trapped by their fears—trapped by the need to see what's around them at all times. That may be fine while you have the choice of keeping the lights on every night, everywhere you go, but what if there's a power outage? How sad, too, that you'll miss out on things like stargazing and camping out, far from where the glow from houses and streetlights can comfort you.

The good news is that it's possible to get over or around fears and phobias, and the fear of the dark is probably one of the easier ones to handle. All you have to do is retrain your brain, and help it to realize that the darkness itself isn't harmful. Sure, the

darkness can hide things that could harm you—things like cliffs, startled bears, and dangerous people. But you also find these things only in certain places. So all you have to do to stay safe in the dark is avoid walking near cliffs, through unknown wilderness, and down deserted streets by night. Alone in your house, the only things in the dark that can hurt you are furniture, toys, electric cables, and other objects you might stumble into. And pretty much the worst that could happen to you is a bump, a bruise, or a stubbed toe. Once you realize that "the dark can't hurt you," it's just a case of getting used to the dark, by immersing yourself in it little by little until you become comfortable.

THE CHANCES

Since the dark itself is not dangerous, it can't really hurt you at all. It is possible, of course, to trip over or fall and hurt yourself in the dark, so you should take care when moving around in it—especially if you're in an unfamiliar place. But even if that does happen, it's the object or the fall that causes the damage, not the dark itself. So while your chances of hurting yourself in the dark are higher than in fully lit places, your chances of being hurt or harmed by the dark are exactly zero!

THE LOWDOWN

Fear of the dark, like most other phobias, is mostly about feeling panicked and out of control. You don't know what's in the dark, and you feel that the only way of regaining control is to switch the lights on to check. But if you think about it, what kinds of things are really likely to be lurking in the dark, waiting to get you? Ghosts? Monsters? Aliens? As we'll see in the next chapter, you have nothing to fear from them. Wild animals? Creepy people? Maybe you would (and should) be worried about those if you were out in the wilderness or on city streets at night, but if you're locked up safe within your own home, then it's very unlikely that anyone or anything could've crept in while you slept.*

So rather than having to switch the lights on, or keep them on all the time, there's another way to regain the feeling of control in the dark. Just try to get used to the dark bit by bit, by gradually making yourself more comfortable with the idea of being in the dark. Psychologists call this "acclimation therapy" or "graded exposure," and it works really well for most people who try it.

If you want to try this, all you have to do is put yourself in a room in semidarkness—as dark as you feel comfortable with, but no more. Then, close the door a little to cut some light from outside (or use a dimmer switch to dim the light in the room). Now you've made it a little darker, just sit and breathe normally until you feel comfortable. If you feel your breathing speed up, try to slow it down by breathing more deeply on purpose. If that doesn't work, turn the lights up a bit until you do feel better, and then try again after a few minutes. Eventually you should be able to extinguish most or all of the light in the room without feeling panicked or nervous. You can take as long as you like to do this—a few days, a few weeks, a month—but most people find the process much easier, and much faster, than they expect.

By getting control of your breathing like this, you can stop the buildup of panic before it begins, and eventually you'll be able to feel in control of your fears and emotions without having to switch the light on to take a peek. You'll be free of your phobia, and you can join the owls, the cats, the moths, and the bats in your fearless friendship with the night!

---

* Unless you have a ninja or a wild animal already living in your house . . . in which case, frankly, you're asking for trouble.

ONE FEAR CONQUERS ANOTHER

I was scared of going to sleep in the dark right up until I was about 10 years old. When I was little, that meant my parents had to leave a small lamp or night-light on when putting me to bed. After a while, though, they began turning the lights off at night to try and get me out of the habit. This worked . . . up to a point. The thing was, I could handle having the room lights off, but I still wasn't comfortable with complete darkness. To avoid panic, I still had to have the hall light on and the bedroom door open a bit to let some light spill in.

Even in my low-lit room I was terrified. Worse yet, my older brother would often go to bed after me and close the door completely. So I would wake up in the middle of the night, panicking in pitch darkness. This went on for quite a while, and for a long time I slept badly every night and woke up tired every morning—literally dragging myself out of bed and into school.

In the end, it was the fear of something else—embarrassment—that got me over my fear of the dark. When I stayed over at friends' houses, I was embarrassed to keep on asking them to "leave the door open a crack" at bedtime, and one friend in particular took great delight in making fun of my "big baby" fear of the dark. So one night I decided to get rid of it—not get over it, just get rid of it, once and for all. And I did.

I went to bed early, switched off the lights, and slowly closed the door. Once in bed, I went through all the same things as usual—jumping at every creaky floorboard and every yowling cat outside. But since I couldn't see anything at all, I couldn't imagine that the crumpled school tie on the floor was an oversized mutant tarantula, or that the bathrobe on the door was actually a hooded madman waiting to strike. So my imagination eventually dried up and gave in, and I drifted off to sleep. I slept soundly that night and woke up feeling rested and proud that I'd managed to conquer my fears after so long. From that day on, I slept in the dark every night.

But, unfortunately, I also needed a new excuse for not wanting to get up for school in the mornings . . .

WATER AND DROWNING

THAT SINKING FEELING

"*Scratching desperately at the tiled side of the pool, I watched tranquil shafts of sunlight waver in the water. I tried to cram my stubby fingertips into the grout of the pool's tiles, trying—and failing—to find some sort of handhold. Alone and sinking downward, a shrill series of screams left my young mouth—but they were lost as soon as they were uttered, transformed into mute bubbles. An eternity later, the heavy water darkened around me. My limbs grew weary from frantic windmilling; my lungs ached; my eyes closed, surrendering. As I choked and sputtered with the sting of chlorine, a hand reached down into the shadowy depths and yanked me upward to the bright air. Gasping and shivering, I realized my savior had been not my mother—who was sitting off to the side of the pool, reading—but the pool's owner.*"

—From "True Stories of Near Drowning," by Erik Henriksen

THE FEAR For many people, drowning is their worst nightmare. In fact, along with being chased and falling, drowning is one of the most common nightmares there is. It's pretty easy to see why. The helpless panic as water fills your mouth, your nose, your throat, and your lungs. The burning pressure in your chest as you try to hold in what little air you have left, hoping against hope that you'll reach the surface in time. Your limbs growing heavier and harder to move. Your body, weighed down with water, sinking further and further from the world above. And the terrible, silent slip into unconsciousness . . .

THE REALITY

Unlike other phobias—like those of animals, needles, and open spaces—the fear of water and drowning (or aquaphobia) turns up in every country and culture, and it is one of the top three most common phobias worldwide.

On some level, everybody fears drowning. If you think you don't, all it will take is one near-drowning experience to show you that you really do. Like the fear of the dark, it's programmed into your brain and nervous system as a healthy warning against putting yourself in mortal danger. But comparing the two, your body's response to drowning is far, far more powerful than its response to finding itself in the dark.

This is because, quite simply, the danger of drowning is so much greater than that of being attacked or injured in the dark. If you're lucky, you can survive in the dark for days, months, or years. But you can't survive for more than a few minutes with your lungs full of water.

To continue living, your brain and body need a constant supply of oxygen. Of course, they need nutrients (or food) and water too, but since your body can store nutrients and water in cells and tissues, it can go days or weeks without those. Oxygen, on the other hand, can't be stored long-term in your body. It gets shifted around and used up very soon after entering your bloodstream, which is why you have to keep breathing—in, out, in, out—nonstop, 24 hours a day, just to stay alive.* Luckily, your body does this automatically and unconsciously—without your having to think about it. Otherwise it'd be tough getting anything else done! With each breath in, oxygen moves from the air in your lungs into

GASP!

* At an average rate of 15 breaths per minute, the average number of breaths we take in an entire lifetime is roughly 400 million. And since we breathe in, on average, about a pint of air per breath, that means we breathe about 53 million gallons of air in a lifetime. That's enough to fill over 300 hot-air balloons! I wouldn't want to try it, though. Air mattresses and swimmies are fine, but trying to inflate an aircraft by yourself is just silly . . .

your blood, and from there it gets carried throughout your body by special proteins called hemoglobins. Once in the cells and tissues, oxygen is used (along with water and carbon-based molecules from food) to create energy. That energy powers every organ and system in your body, including your brain, heart, lungs, kidneys, intestines, and more. In turn, these control your thoughts, your movements, your digestion, and pretty much everything else that keeps you ticking.

Denied oxygen for even a minute, your body quickly burns through its reserves of oxygen from previous breaths, and carbon dioxide builds up in the brain, bloodstream, and lungs. Sensing this, the brain begins to shut parts of itself down (causing you to pass out) as it tries to conserve what little energy-giving oxygen is left. In open air, this often isn't so bad. You may pass out, but there's a good chance you'll recover, provided your air supply is replaced and your breathing restarts. Underwater, the first breath after passing out fills the depths of your lungs with water, stopping any more air from getting through to the bloodstream—even if your unconscious body floats up (or is pulled up by a rescuer) to meet fresh air at the surface.

Knowing this, your body's response to finding itself underwater and without air is a powerful one. Once the low-oxygen, high-carbon-dioxide state is detected, the brain's ancient "fight-or-flight" system kicks in almost immediately, speeding your heartbeat and redirecting more blood to the muscles to help you struggle your way to the surface for more air. Once there, your lungs pull in deep gasping breaths to replace the lost oxygen quickly and return your body to normal.

This is all fine as far as it goes. But the problem is that for an aquaphobic, this system gets triggered early. If you have a true phobia of water, even the thought of putting your head underwater (or of being over water, on a boat or bridge) can trigger the powerful fight-or-flight response. So the person begins to react as if she's drowning—with gasping breaths, flailing limbs, and a pounding heart—when she hasn't even dipped a toe in the water.

Happily, though, death by drowning is actually a pretty rare occurrence, and, provided you're careful in the water, it's unlikely to happen to you. As long as you avoid being caught in a current, caught out of your depth, trapped beneath the surface, or knocked unconscious while in the water, you need never get to the point where you experience the panic of drowning at all. Even for those who do, many are rescued and revived by quick-acting lifeguards and bystanders. Stay smart, and you can enjoy the water in safety. And as with other phobias, even the all-powerful aquaphobia can be overcome.

THE CHANCES

Your odds of drowning depend a little on how strong a swimmer you are, but also on where you find yourself submerged. The odds of drowning in a swimming pool are only about 1 in 7,000, but the odds of drowning in natural water bodies (lakes, seas, and rivers) are more than double that, at around 1 in 3,000.

THE LOWDOWN

As with other instinctive, "primal" fears, the fear of water is an understandable one if you take into account how easily and quickly a body of water can do us in! But if you learn to swim, you understand the dangers, and you have a healthy respect for the water, there's no reason why you can't learn to enjoy traveling, playing, and living with water without panic or dread.

For aquaphobics, learning to swim (or even scuba dive) with a patient, sensitive instructor can be a great way to conquer your fear of water, as long as you take it very slowly, and at your own pace. But if you don't want to go that far, you can at least learn to be more comfortable around the water through acclimation therapy, similar to that used for other phobias.

For everyone who loves (or learns to love) the water, it's still worth bearing in mind that being in and around water can be dangerous if you're not careful and smart about it. For swimming pools, this means

- no swimming alone or unsupervised—so there's always someone to help if something goes wrong
- no running—so that you don't slip, whack your head, and fall in while unconscious
- no diving in shallow water, as hitting your head on the bottom is a pretty bad idea too

That said, swimming pools are still safer than open water sources like lakes, rivers, and seas. This is partly because pools tend to be smaller, shallower, and more closely watched—so if you do get into trouble, it's easier to struggle out and more likely that someone will spot you and come to your aid. But it's mostly also because natural waters are more varied and unpredictable than artificial pools. They may be freezing cold and cause shock and hypothermia. They may hide rocks, discarded fishing nets, and other underwater dangers. And unlike pools, they may have powerful currents and waves. River and coastal sea currents can drag you under, or pull you far from the shore, and a big wave can bash you against rocks or hard against the seabed. So stay safe by the seaside and lakeside by doing this:

- Find out about the water before you plunge in. Is it a known safe spot for swimming? If not, best not to risk it—find somewhere else.
- If it's too rough or choppy, pass. Big waves can be fun, but if they're big enough to toss you into things, it's probably not worth it.
- In the water, take notice of boats, Jet Skis, surfboards, and anything else that might be whipping around nearby. There are often marker buoys to tell you where the boating areas for these begin, so don't stray beyond those and you'll be safer.

And finally,

- Beware of strong currents. It's all too easy for a current to whisk you farther out than you wanted to go before you notice. So keep a close eye on the shore, and you won't find yourself out to sea on your inflatable mattress.

FEAR FACTS:

Children under five and young people aged fifteen to twenty-four have the highest drowning rates. And about 20% of drownings that involve children happen in public swimming pools, with lifeguards present.

It's possible to drown in just 2 inches of water, so people drown not only in seas and swimming pools, but also in bathtubs, buckets, and wading pools.

HEIGHTS, FALLING, AND WIDE-OPEN SPACES

DIZZY HEIGHTS

I happen to have a really bad fear of heights. Trust me—it's no fun at all. When you look down from high up, it feels like you're going to faint, and you just want to get down. If you lean over something and look down, you feel really scared, you go all tingly, and your body automatically pulls you back from the edge. The worst thing is how embarrassing it is. Here are some of my "greatest hits" so far:

1) On our school trip, we had to go up a really high ladder to go rappelling. I was the only one who didn't get up. I got to the tenth step (a new record for me!), but then I had to climb down.

2) When we later went to a ski slope, I was the only one that couldn't get to the top. So I had to ski down from only halfway. . . .

3) I was on a trampoline once (one where you can go really high, wearing a harness around your waist), and I jumped up and . . . wet myself. What a horrible moment!

—Jake M., Wales

THE FEAR

Imagine slipping and tumbling from the roof of a skyscraper, or being sucked out of a speeding airplane,* to find nothing but a few thousand feet of cold air between you and the ground. The air roars past your ears. Your clothes flap and snap against your body as you tumble dizzily in the wind. You stare wide-eyed at the earth far beneath you, as the terrible pull of gravity draws you ever closer toward becoming a crumpled mess (or perhaps just a messy stain) on the ground. Your limbs flail and flap wildly in a hopeless effort to slow your fall. But you are no dainty bird on the wing. You are a big, heavy person. And fall you will . . .

THE REALITY

OK, the fact of the matter is, we humans can't fly. At least not without airplanes or hang gliders.

We're also quite squishy and brittle as animals go, so if dropped from a great height onto a hard surface, even the toughest parts of our bodies will shatter like glass (while the squishiest parts burst like balloons).

Put these two facts together, and you see that we have every reason to fear falling from high places, and every reason to avoid being in high places if we possibly can. Put most people on the roof of a 50-story skyscraper and tell them to stand on the edge and peer down, and you'll see wide eyes, a sharp intake of breath, and a quick retreat back to a safe distance.

But for an acrophobic (someone with an extreme fear of heights), the same reaction might kick in at just 20 inches off the ground rather than 20 stories. What's more, an acrophobia sufferer might also experience vertigo—a dizzying sensation of lost balance that makes the person teeter and wobble like a newborn deer trying to get its balance. Worse still, vertigo doesn't always need a height to happen. It can also be felt by agoraphobics (people who have panic attacks in wide open spaces, shopping malls, supermarkets, or even their own homes) who are firmly at ground level.

So what's going on here? Well, just as with most other phobias, acrophobia and agoraphobia** begin with simple fears that serve a useful purpose, but later grow into uncontrollable states of dread and panic.

---

* I often think about this when using airplane bathrooms. Although I know it's pretty much impossible, I have visions of myself being sucked down the toilet and out of the plane along with the loud WHOOSH! of the vacuum flush. This never happens, of course. Come to think of it, if it did happen, my rear end would probably plug the small drain hole shut anyway . . .

** As these sound so similar, people often mix and combine them when talking about them. But not all agoraphobics are also "acros," and not all acrophobics are "agoros" either. Confusingly, there's also another one called acarophobia, which is the fear of itching. So I guess an agoro-acro-acarophobic would be someone who has nightmares about being in a high-up open space wearing that scratchy all-wool jumper that their auntie bought them for Christmas.

A healthy fear of heights, of course, teaches you to beware the obvious dangers of falling from cliffs, trees, buildings, and other high spots. Everybody, to some extent, is born with this. People who seem fearless of heights—like circus acrobats, Hollywood stunt people, and construction workers who stride along roof beams and scaffolds—have generally unlearned this natural fear of heights by being exposed to heights every day for months or years.

Likewise, many animals (some more than others) fear being caught out in the open, or in places they feel they're unable to escape from, because they know they have nowhere to hide if attacked by a predator. Humans are no exception to this, which is one reason why most of us feel more comfortable surrounded by trees or buildings than we do when surrounded by featureless plains, deserts, or moors. In these "wide open" spaces—even though you can see everything for miles around—you feel exposed and vulnerable because deep down you know you have nowhere to run or hide.

So some acrophobics and agoraphobics simply have more intense (and more easily triggered) versions of fears we all share. They just have stronger emotional responses to heights and places that most of us don't think of as that high, that open, or that dangerous.

But what about the dizziness, wobbling, and falling over? Surely, that's just about the worst thing you could do if you found yourself looking over a high ledge or cliff, right? And how does toppling over help if you find yourself exposed and at risk of attack?

Well, these things don't help. At all. Unlike our basic fear responses, dizziness and wobbling aren't any use when dealing with heights or open spaces. They're the result of a malfunctioning system within the body—one that your brain uses to sense which way up you are, and to maintain your balance.

To keep your body balanced, your brain collects and combines three types of information from the body and its surroundings. The first comes from the muscles, which contain tiny gauges or receptors that detect how stretched out or compressed each muscle is. Putting the signals from these receptors together, the brain can map out where each part of the body is in relation to all the others. This is called proprioception, and it's how you know where your arms, legs, fingers, and toes are even with your eyes closed.

The second type of information comes from the eyes. The eyes take in objects and features of the landscape around you, and the brain uses these as cues to tell, say, which way up you are, and how far you are from the ground and other objects.

The third and final type of information comes from the inner ears, where special fluid-filled organs (called the vestibular organs) sense the pull of gravity, helping you to know which way is up (or rather, down) without having to look or think.

In most healthy people, the brain puts all these pieces of evidence together to build a complete picture of where the body is in space, keeping it upright and balanced. But if you have damaged or altered vestibular organs, then the information from the eyes and ears doesn't always seem to match up, which can confuse the brain and make you feel like you're leaning or toppling over when you're actually standing up straight.

This happens especially when your eyes have trouble judging the distance to the ground—such as when you're very high up. This may explain why many acrophobics

seem to lose their balance when they find themselves up high. But it can also happen when your eyes have trouble judging the distance to the nearest object to you—such as when you're in a wide open, featureless space . . . or in the middle of a cavernous shopping mall, far from the walls and high ceilings. This, in turn, could explain why many agoraphobics topple over in wide open spaces, and feel like they have to cling to walls before they stop feeling dizzy.

THE CHANCES

The odds of being hurt or harmed by (rather than in) an open space, shopping mall, or supermarket are zero. Meanwhile, the average odds of a fatal fall in the United States* look something like this:

- from a ladder or scaffold 1 in 9,000
- from a tall building   1 in 6,500
- from a chair or bed   1 in 5,800
- down stairs or steps   1 in 2,500

AAAAAHHHH!

* Not that the United States is a particularly dangerous place. Once again, it's just where the best records and figures for these sorts of things are kept. So that people can sue each other. Often within seconds of falling.

144

THE LOWDOWN

Like other phobias, acrophobia and agoraphobia can be just extensions of natural fears, or fears left unchecked and running out of control. For people who have full-on panic attacks at heights or in open spaces, acclimation therapy can help them get their fears under control. This could mean taking them to tame heights and spaces and progressing to bigger ones, or it could even mean using virtual reality (VR) programs to get them used to the sensations of being up high or outside before they try it for real. (Phobics with inner-ear problems, though, may also need medicines or special treatment to help relieve their dizziness.)

Ultimately, the good news is that the spaces and heights feared by agoraphobics and acrophobics really aren't, for the most part, very dangerous. In the modern world (rather than the more ancient world of hunters and gatherers), most people have little to fear from being "caught in the open" anymore. And they certainly don't have to worry about being attacked by wild animals in shopping malls and supermarkets. (Well, not the ones I go to, anyway.) So the chances of being harmed or killed in an open space are extremely low. Or at least no worse than anywhere else.

As for heights, it's good, of course, to avoid clambering and skipping around at dangerous heights without climbing ropes and harnesses. Unless of course you're a trained rock climber, a ninja,* or one of those free-running parkour guys who do somersaults off buildings.

Beyond that, just remember that far more tragic plummets and falls happen on household stairs than they do from cliffs, trees, and tall buildings. So the moral of the story is—be careful on the clifftops, but take real care on the stairs!

---

* And even they have to be careful, or risk doing themselves a ninja-ry. Ha-haa!

EXTREME HEIGHTS THERAPY

Despite my successful conquering of "The Dark," my childhood fear of heights lingered on until I was about 16. It wasn't just really high buildings and cliffs either. Basically, being any higher than 6 feet up (and especially being near sheer drop-offs or edges) would make me feel as if my brain was dropping into my knees. When my friends climbed trees I'd do it with them, but I hated every minute of it—feeling dizzy and like I needed to pee throughout the whole experience. When the class went to visit the famous White Cliffs of Dover, near the town where I grew up, I stayed waaaaay back from the cliff edge while the others enjoyed the views of the port, the beaches, and the English Channel below. But unlike being in the dark, I could usually avoid being in high places if I wanted to, so there wasn't such a need to get over this particular fear. So on it went—well into my teens.

Then one day my friend Neil returned from one of those "adventure vacations" in Wales, where he had learned to rock climb, rappel, and more. He was eager to start climbing back in Kent (where we lived) and wanted a partner to go with him. He had all the gear—rope, harnesses, shoes, everything—and was happy to teach me how to use it. I thought about it and decided maybe it was a good time to see if I could conquer my fear of heights. I figured I'd either become a fearless spider-man, or resign myself to avoiding high places for life.

So off we went to the woods, where an old, abandoned railway bridge was used by scout groups to practice climbing and rappelling. It was a red-brick arch bridge about 90 feet tall that spanned a stream valley in the forest.

"We start at the top," said Neil, suiting up in the climbing harness, and tying ropes to trees and himself. "We'll rappel down, then climb back up. That way, it'll be scary at first, but you'll get lower to the ground with every step, and you'll crack your fear of heights before you try to scale it."

That seemed to make sense. "OK—what do I do?" I replied.

"Just watch me first," said Neil, looping a pair of ropes into a steel ring on his belt. "OK—this is your descending line, and it goes through here, and you hold it like this . . . you hold on to this one, no matter what, OK?"

"What happens if I don't?" I whimpered back. "Will I fall?"

"Naaaah," said Neil, grinning, "that's what this other one is for." He grabbed the other rope, and whipped it up and down, sending ripples to the other end, which was fastened to a nearby tree. "This is your safety line. Even if you let go of the first one, this one will stop you from falling. Look—watch this . . ."

And with that, he stepped backward to the edge of the bridge, the hard forest floor yawning away 90 feet beneath him. He began to lean back over the edge, putting his weight on the ropes without holding on with his hands. "See? Safe as houses. It's—wooooaaaaaaaaaaaaaaaaaaaaaaa!" . . . at which point he promptly fell off the edge.

Luckily, though, he'd managed to scrabble a one-handed grip on to the stone edge itself, and I ran forward to grab his arm and help pull him back up.

"Sorry—wrong rope," he said breathlessly. "Let's try that again."

As you might imagine, I wasn't exactly filled with confidence in Neil as a climbing teacher after that. But, incredibly, we did rappel and climb the bridge that day, three times each. And via Neil's unusual brand of "extreme fear therapy," I lost my fear of heights that very day!

TIGHT SPOTS AND CROWDS

BOXED IN AND UP HIGH? NO WAY!

When I was younger, it was my dad who was afraid of things, especially of going into small, tight spaces. I guess he started being claustrophobic when he was a kid, but he still is as an adult. My family went on vacation to St. Louis, where the most famous monument is the St. Louis Arch. It is the tallest national monument in the United States at 630 feet. To get to the top, you have to ride in a tiny, boxlike tram car that seats only five people. It takes 4 minutes to get to the top. When it came time for us to get on the tram, my dad got scared and pointed at my brother, who was only four at the time, and said, "We just can't go on—Brian will be too scared." Sure, blame it on the four-year-old!

—Heather M., United States

THE FEAR

THE FEAR Ahh—claustrophobia. The fear of being trapped in tight or enclosed spaces. Not everyone freaks out at the thought of being trapped in the cold, metal confines of an unmoving elevator. But practically everyone shivers at the thought of being buried alive, or stuck in a dark, damp tunnel, deep under the ground. If that doesn't bother you, how about being crushed within a thick crowd of panicking people, or knocked to the ground and trampled by an angry mob of hundreds or thousands?

If thinking about that makes you tense, then like most people in the world you don't relish the idea of being squashed or suffocated. But if it makes your chest feel tight, your breathing quicken, your shoulders hunch, and your neck shrink inward like a startled tortoise . . . then you are among the world's many true claustrophobes.* And you can probably imagine no worse a fate than being trapped and crushed to death.

THE REALITY

Tight spaces can be dangerous places, and your brain and body know it. So as with heights, wide open spaces, and the dark, the origins of this fear come from a nervous alarm system that evolved in our animal ancestors, helpfully reminding them (and now us) to stay safe.

Understandably, we all show some wariness of being in situations or places where we might be crushed or suffocated. Our bony skulls and rib cages typically do a fine job of keeping the delicate organs inside from being squashed and punctured. But pile enough stuff (or people) on top of us, and our bony crash helmets and chest guards will eventually crack and give way, fatally damaging the brain, lungs, and other organs inside. And we've already seen how little time we can last without breathing, so fear of tight, airless spaces is understandable too. In short: breathing and keeping your proper shape—good; not breathing, or being flattened like a pancake—bad. Very bad.

But while claustrophobia is partly about feeling crushed or suffocated, it's mostly about feeling trapped and unable to escape. This, of course, is understandable too. After all, our animal ancestors didn't want to find themselves trapped and unable to run from predators any more than they wanted to be squashed or suffocated. But very often, serious claustrophobes and melanophobes (people who fear crowds specifically) still have quite a bit of space and breathing room around them when they begin to panic. The walls or crowds aren't closing in—they're just, well, there. And that alone is enough to trigger the feeling of being crushed and suffocated.

As with other phobias, the body's physical "danger" responses

* –phobes and –phobics are two different ways of describing people with phobia conditions. The opposite is –philes, as in aquaphiles (people who like being in the water), aerophiles (people who like flying) and arachnophiles (people who just looove spiders). As my mom always says, "It takes all sorts."

kick in before any real danger is present, causing quickened breathing and tense muscles (especially in the chest, as the rapid panting tires the muscles of the rib cage and diaphragm, which lie around and beneath the lungs). But for claustrophobes, these sensations can feel particularly nasty as their worst fears seem to be coming true. They fear feeling crushed and breathless, and yet the body's own response to that fear leaves them feeling as if their chests are being crushed and their lungs are unable to take in enough air. This will often kick off a cycle of panic and overly rapid breathing (or hyperven-tilation), which

ends only when the claustrophobe escapes the room, space, or crowd* and feels able to move and breathe freely again.

In reality, however, very, very few people meet with injury or doom when trapped in crowds, tunnels, or rogue elevators. And claustrophobia, if left unchecked, can worsen to the point where you can't bear to enter even normal-sized rooms and houses, or face even the smallest crowds of people on the

street. So if you have it, the best thing you can do is try to understand it, to realize that most tight spaces and crowds are not, in fact, dangerous, and to work with a therapist or psychologist until you can get around the "can't escape!" feeling.

THE CHANCES

The odds of being hurt in a tight space vary depending on what kind of space it is, and how far you are from help if you do in fact become trapped. Cabinets and closets, for example, hardly ever suffocate people. So even if, say, an evil younger brother traps you inside one, don't panic—you'll be out again, unharmed, soon enough. This is because cabinets and closets are never completely airtight, and are typically found inside houses, so someone (usually an angry parent) will find you before too long. (And then—ha-haaa!—your little brother is in for it!)

Likewise, elevators, even malfunctioning ones, aren't particularly dangerous places to

---

* Either that or they pass out—which isn't too great in the middle of a rock concert or football crowd either. At worst, you'll be trampled and danced on by people who fail to notice you. At best, you'll wake up covered in sticky soft-drink residue and bits of half-eaten hot dogs.

be. Most elevators aren't airtight either, so you're unlikely to run out of air even if you're stuck in there for hours, or even days. In the United States and the United Kingdom, fewer than ten people a year die in accidents related to elevators, and this almost always involves someone stepping into an empty elevator shaft* rather than being stuck inside the elevator. Being crushed in crowds and trapped in rail or road tunnels is also rare, so they're nothing much to worry about either. The only real risks in tight spaces come from being trapped underground, which can happen if you go caving without proper gear and training, or if you're crazy enough to try "exploring" abandoned mines, tunnels, caves, and building sites by yourself. Every few weeks, some poor kid somewhere dies as a dangerous underground tunnel or construction trench collapses on them. So if the sign says KEEP OUT, take notice—it's there for a reason.

In all, your odds of being in a fatal cave-in or accidental burial are about 75,000 to 1, and your odds of being trapped and running out of air in an enclosed space about 200,000 to 1. So your chances of being hurt in this way are pretty slim, but that doesn't mean you shouldn't be sensible.

* That's an important safety tip—always check that the elevator is actually there before getting on it. Being very smart, I usually do this with horses, trains, buses, and airplanes too. . . .

THE LOWDOWN

Although it might not feel like it to a claustrophobe, small rooms, elevators, train platforms, football games, and rock concerts are all relatively safe places to be, and there's no reason to fear the closeness of walls and crowds, provided they're not getting steadily closer.

If you do suffer from panic attacks in places like this, you can comfortably learn to get around them using the same kinds of therapy exercises that are used for fears of heights and the dark. Little by little, you can learn to control your breathing, your physical responses, and your feelings in ever-tighter spaces and crowds, until they bother you no more. And just as with the fear of heights, you can even try Virtual Reality simulations if jumping straight into the real thing proves too difficult. So you've tried Guitar Hero . . . you've tried Rock Band . . . now try Rock Crowd Hero!

IN THE SPOTLIGHT

WHEN THE TEACHER PICKED ME

Usually I knew the material forward and backward. I could have answered any question standing on my head. If I wasn't so terrified, I suppose I could have even been a show-off. But if she asked me (in front of the whole class), I might as well have been a baboon—the answers would fly out of my head and I would be a stuttering idiot. Sitting there with everybody watching me, the most I could ever say was "I don't know."

—from *Social Phobia*, by John R. Marshall and Suzanne Lipsett

THE FEAR Some of us are fine with the idea of standing in front of huge crowds of people. But others would happily bungee off a 200-foot bridge, or dive into a shoal of circling sharks, rather than experience the sheer terror of facing an audience. Shoved out onstage, or to the front of a class, people like this will quite literally lose their voice. The mouth may open, but the words won't come out. They just stand there gaping like helpless goldfish pulled out of water, their weak limbs quaking with fear, feeling like they want to run, hide, or cry. If that sounds like you, then you are one of the world's many, many sufferers of glossophobia—the fear of speaking (or trying to speak) in public.

THE REALITY

Glossophobia* is amazingly common—there are usually at least four or five kids in every grade who have it, and it's very common in adults too because you generally don't "grow out" of glossophobia. It takes help or practice to get over it. This is because it's basically a type of social phobia—a fear of being watched, judged, or sized up by other people (especially strangers, and especially large numbers of them).

So where does it come from, and what use is it? I mean, if fear of the dark, heights, and dangerous animals helped keep our ancestors from being ambushed, what good is a fear of speaking to people? Wouldn't being able to speak to big groups have helped those early humans to communicate? The ones who were best at it, you'd think, could become chiefs, kings, and emperors.** If speaking is that useful, what is this fear trying to protect us from? Being booed and pelted with rotten vegetables if we do badly?

Well, the answer is—nothing, really. There's no real danger involved in speaking to people. But the action of standing there and being watched can trigger a much older and more useful fear—the fear of being surrounded, threatened, and attacked by other people.

Throughout the animal world, and especially in primates (the group that includes humans, gorillas, and chimpanzees), staring at someone is a signal of fighting or aggression. Even when we chat with people we trust and like, we don't stare them down while we talk. Instead, we shift the focus of our eyes around the other person's face— from their eyes to their mouth and nose and back again—and

---

* Which sounds to me more like "the fear of glossy magazines," or "the fear of shiny paint." But there you go.
** Even today, it's often the best speakers who become politicians, presidents, and prime ministers. Well, with perhaps a few exceptions . . .

we glance away every so often during the conversation. (If you don't believe me, try it with a friend. Sit close to each other and just stare while you talk, without looking away, for one minute. You'll probably find you both start to feel really uncomfortable very quickly!) All of this helps to break up the eye contact, and reassures each person that the other is still friendly. Without it, a long burst of eye contact feels like the buildup to a fight.

Now multiply that one staring pair of eyes by thirty, and you have some idea of why standing up to speak in front of a class can feel so unnerving. Multiply it by 500 or 1,000, and you see why it takes a lot of confidence to be onstage in a packed theater. Even though the audience is (probably) friendly, the sensation is like being surrounded by an angry tribe, and all your brain wants to do is get you out of there. So that's what it prepares you to do. The old "fight-or-flight" system we ran into earlier kicks in, making your heart rate increase,

your breathing tight and rapid, your muscles tense, and your guts feel queasy (as blood is directed away from them). The whole time you're trying to speak or perform, your brain is saying, "OK—any minute now we make a run for it, right? Get ready . . . readyyy . . . readyyyyyyyyyy . . ."

For some people, this feels quite thrilling. But for glossophobics, it's absolutely terrifying.

But if you think about it, there really is nothing to be afraid of this time. Unlike the fear of water, heights, and the dark, there's no real danger present at all. Even if you speak or perform really badly, it's not like the audience is going to kill you—the worst response you'll get is silence, booing, or rotten fruit and veggies. None of these are pleasant, but none of them can actually harm you either.*

Happily, this also makes glossophobia a perfect example of a fear you can beat with simple practice. Since there's no real danger, it's much easier to work up from speaking to one, to two, to ten, to thirty people. Believe it or not, you can go from stage-phobic to star performer in no time!

THE CHANCES

The odds of being killed by a classroom or theater full of people just because you're speaking to or performing for them? Zero. Unless you're really, really bad . . .

No, really—it's zero. Just kidding.

---

* Except perhaps if they throw pineapples. Even a rotten pineapple could give you a nasty bruise if it hasn't been skinned. But thankfully, it's also very difficult to smuggle a whole pineapple into a classroom or theater. Believe me, I've tried.

THE LOWDOWN

The fear of being "in the spotlight" is extremely common and, to those who suffer from it, extremely powerful. But it's also extremely easy to work through, given a bit of effort. Since there's no real danger involved, it's just a matter of convincing your brain that you don't need the "fight-or-flight" system to kick in when you're speaking or performing before people. How do you do that? Practice!

There are lots of ways of working through your fears and building your confidence before audiences. The most direct (and powerful) way is to join a school, church, or community speaking group, where you can be coached on how to give speeches. At first, you may practice alone or with one or two people. Then, as you get more confident, you can work up to larger and larger groups, until before you know it you're speaking to whole school assemblies, church congregations, or community groups! The best thing is that in many cases you get to talk about whatever you want, whether it's "Ten Ways to Make a Better World," "My Love of Dinosaurs," or "Why Xbox Will Always Be Inferior to the Nintendo Wii"!

If that doesn't sound like any kind of fun, then you can get experience with speaking in front of audiences without speaking directly to them. In acting or debating clubs, you can practice talking to small groups of people while being watched by an audience, but without having to look straight at them. Plus the act of concentrating on your lines or on the argument will help distract you from the many watching eyes. When you get really good at it, you might even forget the audience is there!

And if you really can't imagine speaking in front of crowds at all, then you can work up to it (or at the very least gain a lot more confidence) by trying other types of performance instead. Ever wanted to dance? How about play guitar, or sing? Learning a performing art of any kind will help you get over your fears of an audience if you eventually take it to the stage.

So if you're one of the world's many perform-o-phobes, don't worry—the "treatment" for it may turn out to be the most fun you've ever had. The prescription looks like this: take a handful of guitar, acting, or dance lessons, rock a roomful of people with your mad new skills, and call me in the morning!

FEAR FACT:

Famous actor Mel Gibson was so nervous before his first school play that he had to do his role sitting down. His legs and body were too weak for him to stand.

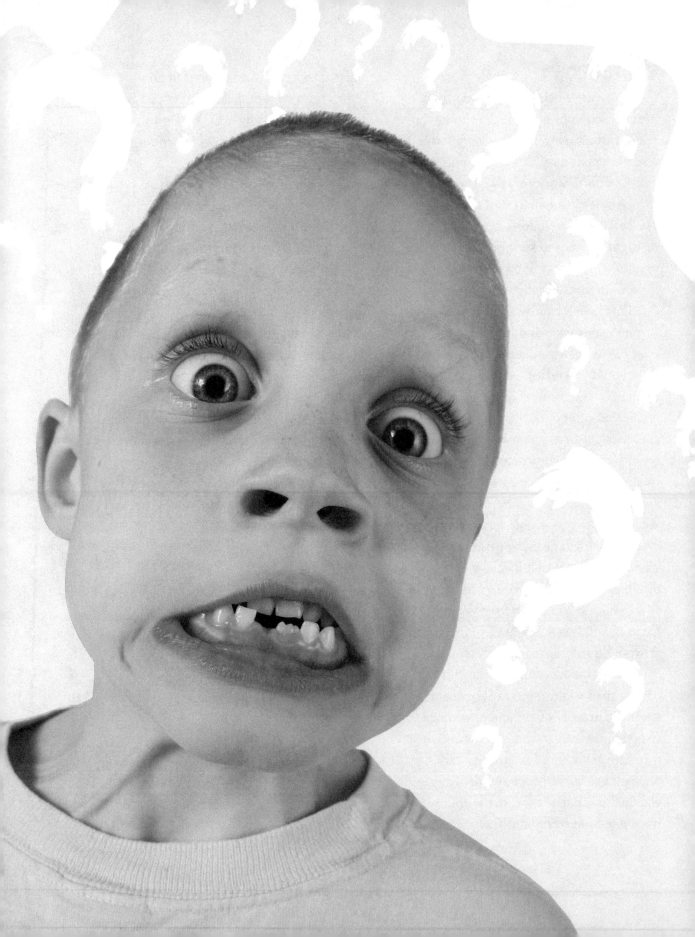

CHAPTER 6
THE UNKNOWN

FEAR OF FEAR ITSELF

So we've worked out that people are afraid of lots of different things for lots of different reasons. A few fears are built into our brains from birth to help protect us from harm. We learn most of the rest through scary experiences of our own, or from hearing scary stories from others. But the one thing that ties almost all of these fears together is . . . uncertainty or not knowing.

If someone moves a hand slowly toward your face, you just sit there and watch the person do it. But if someone sneaks up on you and quickly passes a hand in front of your face from behind, you flinch.

Why? Because it happened too quickly for your brain to work out what was going on. For the first split second after the hand appears, your brain doesn't know if it's a hand, a bird, or a flying rock in your face. So it triggers an automatic reaction—your flinch reflex—to quickly jerk your head away (and shield your eyes, partly or fully closing them) until it has had a chance to work out what you're dealing with. So this reflex is a kind of automatic fear, lasting a fraction of a second, that kicks in when your brain doesn't know what's going on.

A similar thing happens if you slowly place a fake spider on someone's leg while he or she watches. Unless they're seriously arachnophobic, hardly anyone would flinch or jump if they saw you do this. But place it there while they're not looking, and even someone who likes spiders may jump and hastily brush it off. Again, in the first split second after spotting it, the brain can't work out how it got there, or exactly what it is (a fake spider or a real one). So the person jumps and swats at it as an automatic response to something unexpected and unknown. The same thing happens with sudden loud bangs, with sudden bursts of music in horror movies, or with sudden flashes of movement at the edge of your vision.* "Whawuzzthat?!?!" your brain says. And until it gets an answer, flinching and fear are the standard responses.

In a way, all fear responses share this link to uncertainty and not knowing. But while flinching happens in a fraction of a second, anxiety, dread, and panic are reactions to the unknown that can build up over minutes, hours, days, or years.

Once the flinch response is over, a person's reaction will depend on what he knows and how he feels about spiders. Arachnophobes, not knowing whether or not the spider on their leg (or—if they've just brushed it off in a panic—on the floor) is venomous or whether it will jump at them, may immediately panic or become hysterical as a second, more powerful fear response kicks in. But an arachnophile—who knows it isn't dangerous, and won't jump—may not panic at all.

Most people, perhaps, would be somewhere in the middle. Not certain whether the spider is dangerous (but noticing it isn't jumping or trying to bite

* It also works with hamsters placed carefully on the heads of balding uncles. I did this once to my Uncle Eddie at a family party as he sat and chatted with my Uncle Peter on the sofa. Peter didn't see me put my pet hamster on there, but he jumped out of his skin when Eddie's "wig" leaped off his head and scurried across the carpet. Which got a good laugh out of pretty much everyone in the room.

them yet), they may be nervous or anxious, but not terrified. The only difference among the three people is how much they know about the spider, and how uncertain they are about what's likely to happen next.

The fears in this final section are special, as they all relate to things that are scary mostly because they're unknown or unknowable. Spiders, earthquakes, lightning, dentists, and diseases can be pretty scary, but at least we know and understand what they are. Not so for ghosts, monsters, aliens, death, and dying. These things are, for many people, mysterious and difficult to understand. They sit within the "Big Book of Scary, Bad Stuff"* that has confused and terrified people for thousands of years. But if you think about it, earthquakes, lightning, and many other things were, until fairly recently, in that book too. Before we had science to help explain what these things were, people thought they were the work of demons, evil spirits, or angry gods. Now that we know more about earthquakes and lightning, we don't fear them nearly as much. We might not be able to predict when they'll strike, but we know why they happen, and we know they're not trying

to get us, even when they do.

Now here's the funny thing. Our brains make us fear things we don't recognize, can't expect, or don't understand. But as we've already seen, learning more about the things we fear can help us understand them and, eventually, lose our fear of them altogether.

So being afraid of something just because you don't understand it—but then refusing to try to understand it—is like being afraid of fear itself!

So let's try and take a few more things out of that "Big Book of Scary, Bad Stuff" as we head into the final chapter and deeeeeep into . . .

. . . the unknooooown.

---

* This book doesn't really exist, of course. Although that is a great title . . .

MONSTERS

THE TERRIBLE TURTLE MONSTER

In Japan, people still speak of the Kappa, a strange monster that looks like a cross between a monkey, a frog, and a turtle. About the height of a small child, it swims like a fish in water, but on land it walks upright on webbed feet, like a human. Weirdest of all, it has a bowl-like dent in the top of its head filled with water—the source of its enormous strength and power.

Some Kappa, it's said, are truly evil. They kidnap children and eat people, sucking their victims' entrails out through their bottoms. The best way to defeat a Kappa is to bow to it, as all Kappa (even the evil ones) are very polite and will bow back, spilling the precious, strength-giving water from the pool on top of their heads.

THE FEAR

As scary as lightning, spiders, dentists, and darkened rooms can be, at least we know what they are. Monsters, on the other hand, are different. They might be animals, they might be mutant people, but we don't really know what they are. (If we did, then we could call them something else, like a bear, a dinosaur, or a big, hairy person.) And that makes them scarier than anything.

Thousands of mysterious beasts and monsters have been sighted all over the world, and they seem to date back as far as human history itself. There are humanlike monsters with huge, hairy bodies and terrifying strength. There are batlike monsters that swoop out of the night to suck the blood of animals and children. Ship-sinking sea monsters with writhing tentacles, man-eating dog-beasts with terrible fangs, hideous cat-beasts with horrible claws . . . the list goes on and on. Scientists say most monsters are just figments of our imaginations. But with so many monsters spotted in so many places, so many times, how can they be sure? Who's to say there really isn't something lurking under your bed, waiting to eat you just as soon as you nod off to sleep?

THE REALITY

Who's to say there isn't a monster under your bed? Well, me for starters. And pretty much every scientist in the world.

It's true that scientists don't know everything (and they don't pretend to either—one of the great things about science is that it allows you to be happily uncertain about things). But what they do know is based on proof and evidence. And as far as monsters go, there just ain't much of either.

What little evidence there is for monsters tends to be pretty sketchy—usually a grainy, out-of-focus photograph or a set of footprints indicating that the monster was just here, and you just missed it. Most monster "proof" comes in the form of stories or eyewitness accounts from people who have seen them. Now you could say that's proof enough for you, but, for scientists, this isn't really good enough. Poor-quality, grainy photographs and tracks make it unclear whether you've captured evidence of a monster or a normal animal (or person) under weird lighting conditions.

Take, for example, the Yeti, otherwise known as the Abominable Snowman. Huge, hairy man-ape creatures like

this have been talked about for centuries, in countries all over the world. In Asia, it's called the Yeti. In North America, it's called Bigfoot (or Sasquatch), in South America the Ucu. Even Australia (where you'd think it'd be a bit warm for hairy man-apes), there's one called the Yowie. In the past, some scientists thought that maybe there was some truth to the stories. Maybe these beasts were really the prehistoric, prehuman survivors of another age—massive hairy cavemen who never died out. But after years of searching and collecting evidence, all we've turned up are blurred photographs that could easily be

SNORT!

normal people (possibly in fake Yeti suits!) or huge footprints in snow and mud that could simply have enlarged as they decayed, the edges falling inward over time to give the illusion of a huge footprint.

Similarly, some scientists used to think the famous Loch Ness Monster might be a plesiosaur—a huge aquatic reptile* that somehow survived in a Scottish loch (lake) for millions of years after all the others had died out. Maybe they even survived in lakes elsewhere too, since Nessielike monsters have also been reported in lakes in Africa (where it's called the Mokele-mbele) and China (home of the "Heavenly Lake Monster"). But in the absence of anything but stories and blurry photographs that could be fins, which is more likely? That families of massive reptiles have survived almost unseen since the Cretaceous Period, or that the locals are mistaken?

* But not—as many people think—a dinosaur, although they died out around the same time as most of the true dinosaurs. Pterosaurs aren't dinosaurs either. Or rather, weren't dinosaurs, since they're gone too. Sadly.

Now you could say, "OK—so there's no evidence yet, but that doesn't mean there never will be." That's true. Science never rules out the possibility that monsters exist. And it could be that some so-called monsters are really just animals that we already know about (but the locals don't), or even rare species we've never seen before. In both cases, eyewitness sightings of these "monsters" might be exaggerated because they're so unusual and difficult to explain. Experiencing the unknown can play tricks on your senses and memory, making things seem bigger (and scarier) than they really are.

So some monsters may just be normal animals, others may be hoaxes or tricks created on purpose to fool people, and perhaps most are just stories made up to explain unusual events (like escaped zoo animals killing livestock, or strange tracks formed in snow or mud by wind and weather).

THE CHANCES

Since monsters are either imagined, created by hoaxes, or not actually monsters at all, then your chances of being hurt or killed by a monster are pretty much exactly ZERO. I say "pretty much" because it's possible that your "monster" could turn out to be something like an escaped big cat— and one of those could certainly do you damage. But then it's not really a monster that's attacking you, is it? It's . . . well . . . a cat. In any case, escaped cats don't generally hide under beds or in closets, so you're still in the clear.

THE LOWDOWN

Whether imagined, faked, or just a case of mistaken animal identity, we can safely say that monsters are not a threat to your health or survival. Even if (and this is a big "if") some "monsters" turn out to be huge, dangerous animal species that we thought were extinct—like dinosaurs, pterosaurs, and saber-toothed tigers—then they're probably still not much of a danger to you. Think about it: if it's been that hard to catch a glimpse of these beasts over decades and centuries, then it's pretty unlikely that you'll just stumble upon one . . . or have one stumble upon you.

In the Himalayas, you've far more to fear from freezing to death and falling down crevasses than from a ravenous Yeti. And if you ever meet one, you can tell him I said that.

THE LOCH NESS MONSTER Reported sightings of the world-famous Loch Ness Monster (or "Nessie," as the locals call her) date back almost 2,000 years. But interest in Nessie really peaked in 1972, when a diver captured what looked like a plesiosaur's flipper in an underwater photograph. Then in 1987 a team of scientists used nineteen boats with sonar scanners to sweep the loch looking for her. Alas—no luck and no proof. But since they left a good third of the loch unscanned, the locals say Nessie (or a family of Nessies) could still be there, hiding.

THE YETI This 8-foot-tall, shaggy, gray man-ape has apparently been roaming the mountain passes of Nepal and Tibet for centuries, and the Himalayan Sherpa people know and fear the Yeti (or rather, Yetis, as they believe there are many of them) as an evil spirit. European mountain climbers have also reported spotting Yetis or Yeti footprints on icy glaciers and peaks never before climbed. But beyond a few sketchy footprint photographs, there's no solid, hairy evidence of them yet.

THE BEAST OF BODMIN This large leopard—or pantherlike cat—has been spotted thousands of times a year by the residents of Bodmin Moor in Cornwall, in southwest England. The beast is said to roam the moor year-round, killing hundreds of sheep and cows. Sightings of footprints, dead livestock, and the animal itself date back only to the 1980s, and some think it's possible that the "Beast" is actually a family of big cats that was released into the wild by a private owner around that time. One piece of video evidence does exist, showing a distant, dark, pantherlike animal stalking the moor. But no one has ever seen the Beast of Bodmin ("Bob" to his friends) up close, let alone captured it.

THE KRAKEN This enormous squidlike sea monster, thought to be between 50 and 200 feet long, has terrorized the seas of northern Europe since Viking times. Scientists used to dismiss the Kraken as a complete myth, but since the recent discovery of a new species of giant squid—the colossal squid—many are not so sure. Colossal squid may reach up to 50 feet in length, and a "baby" specimen measuring 33 feet and weighing almost 1,000 pounds was captured by a fishing boat near Antarctica in 2007.

THE AHOOL Named after their shrieking cry, Ahools reportedly look like monkeys with massive, 14-foot-wide bat wings. They are said to live in caves in the rain forests of Indonesia, and locals say they swoop out at night to catch fish in their clawlike hands. Many scientists think these may be exaggerated sightings of flying foxes—large, furry bats that live in the region.

THE KONGAMOTO Another huge batlike creature, this time living in Zambia, Africa. Locals say it has a hairless, reptilian body and a long beak with teeth (much like the now-extinct pterodactyl). They also say that it swoops down on fishermen and capsizes their boats, and causes death to anyone who looks into its eyes. But there's no real evidence of a pterosaur—or a flying-bat monster—living in Africa.

THE BUNYIP The Australian Aboriginal people say the Bunyip—a large doglike creature with webbed feet and walruslike tusks—lives in riverbeds and watering holes throughout the bush, coming out at night to eat any animal that comes near. No real-live Bunyips have yet been found, and most zoologists doubt it exists. But then again, they also doubted the existence of the platypus, which was painted and talked about by Aboriginals for generations before skeptical scientists finally found one.

THE CHUPACABRA This bear-sized, lizard-skinned, dog-faced, snake-fanged vampire lives in South America, where it sucks the blood from pigs, horses, and goats. Oh, and it also has porcupine quills down its back and hops like a kangaroo. Most zoologists consider this one waaaaay too weird to exist—and there's certainly never been any evidence of it, other than livestock that could easily have been killed by other animals (or people) instead.

THE MONGOLIAN DEATH WORM An enormous blood-filled worm that is supposed to live in the dunes of the Mongolian desert. It can kill you by spitting venom at you, or by shocking you like an electric eel. None has ever been found by zoologists. Possibly because they've all been eaten by mutant Mongolian blackbirds. But, hey—that's just my theory.

THE MOTHMAN A 7-foot-tall humanoid monster with huge moth wings and glowing red eyes, sighted in parts of West Virginia since the 1960s. Some say it's an evil spirit. Others say it's a failed experiment—an evil mutant animal escaped from a local army base. I say the locals should eat less cheese before bed.

ALIENS

THE WORLD'S FIRST ALIEN ABDUCTION?

Shortly after 10 p.m. on September 19, 1961, American vacationers Betty and Barney Hill were driving home from their trip to Canada. Suddenly, they both noticed a bright star that appeared out of nowhere and seemed to be following them. Barney thought it might be an airplane or satellite, but when the light remained Betty grabbed a pair of binoculars to view the object, and Barney stopped the car for a closer look. It appeared to be a large, glowing pancake with a double row of windows.

Then Barney noticed there were others looking at them through the windows and became terrified, convinced somehow that he and Betty were about to be captured. They raced off, accompanied by a "beeping" sound from behind the car, which seemed to make them drowsy. After a second burst of the beeping sound, they became fully awake, and found themselves several miles away from where they had spotted the object. Unable to remember what had happened, they drove home.

Shortly after the UFO incident, Betty began having nightmares in which she was taken aboard the UFO and examined by little humanoid beings, while Barney began to suffer from exhaustion, high blood pressure, ulcers, and a strange ring of warts near his groin. . . .

THE FEAR

Since the first reports in the late 1960s, there have been millions of accounts of people being abducted by aliens. The victims are usually either hijacked outside their homes by UFOs or taken from their beds in the middle of the night. These alien kidnap victims (or "alien abductees") often remember very little of what happened, recalling only later how they were taken inside spaceships, injected with needles, and poked and prodded by alien "doctors." Many recall waking up in their beds, paralyzed, to find hideous creatures standing before them.

Creatures with huge heads and eyes, spindly limbs and grayish skin, watching them with silent, evil curiosity.

What do they want? Are they scouts leading an invasion of our planet? Are they conducting some bizarre alien experiment on us all? Are they creating a race of freakish alien–human half–breeds? Whatever the case, it seems we puny humans are no match for their superior technology and intelligence. Their spaceships fly around undetected by armies and air forces. They control our minds and our bodies, plucking us from our homes at will. And we're powerless to understand or resist. So run for your lives—the body-snatchers are coming!

THE REALITY

OK, OK, calm down. They're not coming just yet. In fact, they may never come, and there's very little evidence that they've ever been here at all.

Despite the millions of alien abduction stories that have surfaced over the last half-century, not one has provided a scrap of solid evidence that it ever happened. No alien souvenirs swiped from spaceships, no photographs or video footage of their captors, and no outside witnesses to back up stories. So all we have to go on are the victims' own words and memories. What little "evidence" has been offered so far has been sketchy at best. Blurred photographs of

Frisbee-like objects or wobbling lights in the sky, strange bruises and marks on the bodies of alien abductees, and so on. Looked at like this, which seems more likely: that evil aliens are kidnapping people all the time, largely unnoticed by the rest of us, or that these "alien kidnap" victims are misleading us (or themselves)?

That's not to say that aliens definitely don't exist. Having no proof isn't the same thing as proving there's nothing there. In fact, given the unimaginably huge size of the universe, and the number of planets in it that could support life (scientists estimate that there could be thousands of suitable planets in our galaxy alone), it would be surprising if it turned out we were all alone. But while there might well be life elsewhere in the universe, it might not be complex life like us. For almost all of the Earth's 4.5-billion-year history, all that lived here were simple, single-celled organisms like bacteria—complex life only evolved within the last few hundred million years. So if we do find life elsewhere, there's a good chance it won't be at the same stage of evolution as life on Earth. Or to put it another way, life could be common, but complex life like humans could be very rare—even unique—in the universe.

Even assuming there was complex life out there somewhere on another planet, that's not to say they have civilizations and technology, or spacecraft. We humans only came up with those things within the last few thousand years (for manned spacecraft, only about 50 years ago, and only a few of those have ever made it more than a few miles away from Earth). What's more, we already know there are no alien civilizations in our solar system, and the nearest solar systems capable of supporting them are billions and trillions of miles away. So even if "they" are out there, it's unlikely that alien civilizations would manage to bridge the distance between us to come and visit. (And if they had, then you'd think after all that effort getting here they might do something a bit more useful than kidnapping American farmers at random.)

Of course, that doesn't necessarily mean all of the so-called alien abductees are lying, or that all UFO sightings are hoaxes. Many (if not most) alien abduction stories can be explained by medical conditions like temporal lobe epilepsy and sleep paralysis. Both of these conditions can make victims feel as if they're paralyzed and trapped inside their own bodies. They can also make sufferers hallucinate (or seem to see, as if in a waking dream) humanoid figures right in front of them, and interfere with memory formation so that it seems like the person has "lost" minutes or hours of their lives (which in reality they just can't remember).

Even for those who don't suffer from these conditions, many otherwise normal people often experience hallucinations just as they drift off to sleep (hypnogogic hallucinations), or just after waking up (hypnopompic hallucinations). At these times, the brain becomes more suggestible and prone to confusion—which is the very thing hypnotists exploit when they make people sleepy and get them to do funny things on stage. In fact, many abductees (including Betty and Barney Hill, whom we met in the opening story) actually "recall" their alien encounters under hypnosis, which can create a very unreliable mixture of real and imagined memories.

So while some "alien victims" are hoaxers and liars, perhaps most actually believe that it really happened to them—for reasons they don't themselves understand.

Happily, this means that neither they, nor we, need to fear an alien attack any time soon

THE CHANCES

If you believed every alien abduction report was true—and there are thousands of them every year in the United States alone—then you'd have to accept that about 2% of the world's population is "taken" by aliens annually. That's well over a hundred million people. As the late, great astronomer Carl Sagan once said, "You'd think someone would have noticed all that UFO traffic."

But since there's no proof that alien abductions have ever happened, your chances of being kidnapped, harmed, or killed by aliens are—as far as we know—precisely zero. Hooray!

THE LOWDOWN

Based on all the evidence we have, aliens may well exist somewhere in the universe, but none have been here yet. So until the day an advanced alien civilization does surprise us by arriving in a mothership to claim the planet for themselves, we can safely say that aliens are nothing to be afraid of.

All those scary alien abduction stories can be explained by a simple fear of the unknown, combined with mistakes, hallucinations, medical conditions, and the influence of books, movies, and the media.

"Abduction" stories didn't start with aliens either. Throughout history, there have been stories of children and adults being "taken" or attacked by demons or monsters. These stories share many of the same features as those of alien abductees—such as being "attacked" in bed, in the middle of the night, being paralyzed or frozen, and being taken up into the sky. All that has happened is that aliens have become the new demons—a newer, more modern way to explain the same feelings of fear and powerlessness that people get when they see a strange light they can't explain, or half-wake from a dream to find themselves unable to move.

Ever since the 1960s, books, movies, and the media have helped spread common ideas of what aliens might look like and how they might behave. All over the world, people report seeing the same kinds of gray, spindly, big-eyed aliens because that's how the earliest stories of the 1960s described them. Alien attack stories are like high-tech, modern monster myths that have spread around the world, becoming folktales for everyone who has seen the movies or read the books. All of these ideas just give a name and a shape to our shared fear of the unfamiliar and unknown.

So don't worry—the alien body-snatchers aren't coming to get you. At least not yet . . .

FAMOUS HOLLYWOOD ALIENS

E.T. (from *E.T.—The Extra-Terrestrial*) A small, brown, wrinkly alien with a glowing finger, healing powers, and an extendable neck. Looks a lot like a vacuum cleaner with eyes. Which could be confusing for them, if aliens like this ever came to Earth.

CHEWBACCA (*Star Wars*) A tall, hairy member of an alien race called the Wookies, who hangs out with Han Solo on his spaceship. Can understand English, but only replies in growls and gurgles.* Looks a lot like a tall man in a hairy suit. If the world were invaded by Wookies, we'd soon run out of shampoo.

XENOMORPHS AND PREDATORS (*Alien, Aliens, Alien 3, Predator, Predator 2, Alien vs Predator . . .*) One is a huge, hideous, parasitic monster that eats people's brains and incubates its young inside human bodies. The other is a dreadlocked, crab-faced, stealth-suited killer that hunts humans for sport. If these things exist, we'd better hope they never find us!

THE MARTIANS (*War of the Worlds*) Small, squishy, large-headed aliens with superior intelligence and technology to ours. They stride around in huge war machines, exterminating humans with heat rays, while keeping a few of us in reserve to harvest our blood. Luckily, common Earth bacteria are deadly to them. Let's hear it for the bacteria—yet again!

MISTER SPOCK (*Star Trek*) An extremely clever, humanlike alien with pointy ears and odd-looking eyebrows. His mother was human, but his father was from an alien race called the Vulcans. He has superhuman strength, he can read minds, and he can knock people out by pinching them. Would be a great friend to have at school, since he could do your math homework and fend off bullies. Fantastic.

* Which, confusingly, Han Solo seems to understand perfectly. Perhaps he took Wookie language classes at some point.

GHOST'S

THE HAUNTED TOWER

Today the Tower of London is one of the most popular tourist destinations in Europe. The central tower is almost 1,000 years old and was built by order of William the Conqueror to celebrate his victorious conquest of England in 1066. Since that time it has been expanded, fortified, and used by various monarchs as a fortress, a palace, and a prison. It is also a place of death—hundreds of prisoners have been executed within its walls, the last as recently as 1940. Little wonder, then, that the tower has also been the location of more ghost sightings and encounters than perhaps any other place in the world.

In 1483 two young princes were murdered in the tower, and their ghosts were said to haunt it until their bones were discovered in 1674 and reburied in Westminster Abbey. One of King Henry VIII's more unfortunate wives, Anne Boleyn, was beheaded in the tower courtyard, as was the treasonous Guy Fawkes. Their spirits, too, are said to walk the grounds. A mysterious "White Lady" waves at visiting schoolchildren from windows, and terrified tower guards once spoke of an evil presence that attacks lone patrollers by night. The invisible specter, it was said, caused a crushing sensation in your chest, or tried to strangle you with your own clothes. At least one guard reportedly died of shock when he encountered it . . .

THE FEAR

Ooooooooo, creepy! There's nothing like a good ghost story to get your heart beating faster and send chills down your spine. And there are certainly plenty of stories out there to choose from. There are stories about haunted houses—with creepy noises, creaking doors and furniture shifted by an invisible presence. Stories about séances—where psychic mediums fall into trances and become possessed by the ghosts of the dead, while the table shakes and the room lights flicker frighteningly on and off. Stories about curious kids who play with Ouija* boards, asking questions of evil spirits—who toy with them . . . and tell them only of their own deaths.

Worst of all, there are stories of actual ghost sightings. Horrible apparitions with dead, lifeless eyes and grasping hands. Spirits seeking revenge for their untimely deaths. Floating phantoms who haunt the hallways of places where they once lived. Ghastly specters who sob, scream, and scare the poor living to death—where they join the ghostly hordes and live on in limbo to terrify us all. *WOOOOOOOOOO!! WOOOOOO-OOOOOOO-OOOOOOOO . . .*

THE REALITY

. . . OOOOOOOO!!! WOO-OO—

(Cough.) Ahem! All right, enough of that.

As fears go, ghosts are a funny one. We love to scare ourselves with stories about them, yet most of us won't admit we really believe in them. Not really.

But then where do all those stories come from? It seems difficult to ignore all those creepy stories when there are so many of them out there, unexplained . . .

Few of us have ever had a ghostly encounter ourselves, yet everyone seems to know someone who has. There are those who say they've seen one or heard one clunking around their house or floating through their bedroom. There are those who have been to see mediums, or fooled around with Ouija boards, and say they were convinced they were communicating with the dead. Then there are books and movies about ghosts and hauntings—all "based on a true story." And what about all those programs on TV where real-life "ghost hunters" visit haunted places, capturing strange, ghostly happenings on night vision cameras and special spirit-sensing instruments?

---

* Although most people call these "Ouiji" or "Wee-jee" boards, the correct name is actually "Ouija." They get their name from the French and German words for "yes"("oui" and "ja") since in addition to the letters of the alphabet, all Ouija boards also display the words "yes" and "no," so that the ghost/spirit/person pushing the glass can answer simple questions. The wittiest ghosts typically answer "Is there anybody theeeerrre?" with a "No."

Stick all this together, and there seems to be quite a lot of evidence for ghosts and spirits, and plenty of fuel for the widespread fear of them—otherwise known as phasmophobia. But how well does the evidence really hold up?

The truth is, just as with monsters and aliens, there are plenty of stories, but the evidence doesn't hold up well. In fact, in over a century of research into parapsychology (the study of psychic abilities and life after death, using sciencelike methods), there is no proof that ghosts and spirits exist. Of course, that doesn't mean we've proven that ghosts don't exist either. But since we can explain most of these scary goings-on in other ways, we're pretty sure that there's no real reason to be afraid of them.

Time and time again, scientists have demonstrated that mediums (people who claim they can talk to spirits or the dead) are

either fakes or—at the very least—failures. When mediums hold "sittings" or "readings" with those who have lost a loved one, they often give details of the dead person's life— guided, they say, by the spirits of the dead themselves. But while their "readings" might seem accurate to the listener, they're actually using clever word tricks and clues to guess the details. For example, the medium might begin like this:

"I see a red bicycle, the letter 'K,' and a young woman . . ."

"Well," says the listener, "my mother's sister was called Catherine, but I don't think she rode a bike . . ."

"Yes, yes—Catherine. She's here now. And she did have a bicycle when she was younger—you were just too young to remember. I'm also seeing a black dog . . . or possibly a cat."

"That's amazing!" says the listener, "Aunt Catherine did have a cat—a big black one! And now that you mention it, I think she and my mother did ride bikes when they were little . . ."

So the listener sees "the letter 'K'" as a correct guess at "Catherine," even though the medium was actually wrong about it! And the chances of the listener knowing someone connected to her late mother whose name began with either a "C" or a "K" are pretty high. Likewise, since most people ride bikes when they're young, and most people keep pets, the chances that this person "used to ride a bicycle" and had a "dog . . . or possibly a cat" are very high too. In strict tests, scientists have shown that a medium's guesses are no better than anyone else's. They're wrong at least as often as they're right. So if they're not faking their chats with the dead, then they're really not very good at it.

As for séances and Ouija boards, they don't hold up well to strict testing either. The wobbling table in a séance isn't caused by a ghost, but by the host lifting it with a foot (or sometimes using a special "hands-free" body harness) from underneath, and lights flicker because the host has set up special switches to trigger them. Ouija boards, on the other hand, spell out answers because one or more people touching the glass are pushing it (whether they realize it or not) toward certain letters. The movement is caused by a mind trick called the ideomotor reflex,* not by some mischievous poltergeist.

Finally, we have the full-on ghostly visits, visions, and hauntings. How do we explain those? Well, not one case that has ever been seriously investigated has given any permanent evidence that a ghost was present. Sometimes people will report seeing, hearing, or feeling similar things in the same places. But they always fail to capture any photographs, sound recordings, or video clips that will back up the story. Which seems to suggest that the ghostly sights, sounds, and sensations may be in the haunted head rather than the haunted house . . .

Just as with alien abduction stories, there's some evidence that medical conditions such as temporal lobe epilepsy can cause hallucinations that make it look as if there are strange people in the room. So where some people with this condition see "aliens," others see "ghosts."

Some researchers have also found that strong electromagnetic fields can make people—even people without temporal lobe epilepsy—hallucinate by affecting the normal workings of their brains. Certain electrical waves, applied to certain parts of the brain, can make you feel as if there's someone standing beside you, or even touching you. So it may be that many "haunted" houses are just old houses with old, sketchy electrical wiring that floods certain spots of the house with electromagnetic fields. If you walk into that spot, your brain gets affected, and you "see" or "feel" the ghost.

* See page 177 for how you can test this out for yourself—it's great for freaking out your friends!

There is even a type of sound that can cause your eyeballs to vibrate and make it look as if there's a hazy, floating shape at the edge of your vision. This type of sound, called infrasound, has a frequency too low for us to hear,* so it affects us without our realizing it. Infrasound can be created in a number of different ways, including by the massive wind turbines used to generate electricity. So if this theory is correct, maybe ghost "sightings" will go up along with all the new windmills we're building!

In any case, all of these explanations seem more likely than the alternative—that evil spirits linger on after death to terrorize us, but leave no evidence beyond a few sketchy ghost stories.

THE CHANCES

The odds of being dragged into the land of the dead by a ghost or evil spirit—as far as we know—are nil. You could, of course, scare yourself (or someone else) to death if you (or they) had a heart problem, but you couldn't blame that on a ghost. Not even if you were dressed like one.

THE LOWDOWN

Ghosts, as far as we know, simply do not exist and pose no danger to you, me, or anyone else. Ghost sightings and stories are just another example of people seeing, hearing, or feeling things they can't easily explain and slapping a "supernatural" label on it to try and make sense of it all.

Some ghostly sensations can be explained by simple trickery, others by medical conditions like temporal lobe epilepsy, and still others by the rare (but real) effects of electromagnetic fields and soundwaves on the eyes, ears, and brain. Whatever the case, ghosts are best thought of as hallucinations and tricks of the mind, rather than evil forces out to get us.

It's easy to be freaked out by something you don't expect and can't easily explain. But that doesn't mean you have to stay freaked out. Look a little deeper, and you'll almost always find a simple explanation for the eerie knocking sound you heard in the walls, the cold shiver you felt as you stood in that cellar, or the blurred face you're sure you saw at the window of that deserted house. Instead of giving in to your panic and your fear of the "unknown," think about it or investigate a little more. Chances are you'll soon find that the real explanation—a swelling metal pipe in the walls, a draft of cold air in the cellar, or a weird lighting effect in the window—isn't scary at all.

* Whales and elephants, however, use infrasound to communicate all the time. So either their eyeballs are vibration-proof, or they're constantly seeing ghosts and freaking each other out. If so, I wonder what whale and elephant ghosts look like? Would they have trunks, or flippers and tails? Hmmmmmm . . .

"Poltergeist" is a German word meaning "knocking ghost." These mischievous spirits are famous for making knocking noises and moving things around in people's houses. Some people also believe that spirits move the upturned glass on a Ouija board. On a Ouija board, everyone touches the glass but no one pushes it—yet the glass, spookily, moves itself, as if possessed by a poltergeist.

In truth, the glass-touchers are pushing—they just don't know it. Just by looking at a letter on the board, one of the touchers begins to push the glass unconsciously toward it. Then, as the glass moves toward the letter, the others help propel it and stop it, because they're unconsciously reacting to the first toucher's motion.

In certain circumstances, if you think about a movement and you're relaxed, the movement becomes real as your body responds in tiny ways you can hardly detect. This is called the ideomotor reflex.

You can test it with a pendulum. A necklace with a heavy pendant will do nicely. Or, failing that, a chestnut tied on a string. It doesn't really matter as long as it can swing freely.

Wrap the string or chain around the base of your middle finger, then raise your elbow to shoulder level and hold the pendulum over a table so that the pendant, chestnut, whatever doesn't touch the surface. Now try to keep your hand as still as you can, but at the same time, look at the pendant and imagine it moving to and fro. First try left to right—keep your hand still but keep thinking about it. Eventually the pendant will start to move just as you imagine it. Now imagine it stopping. It will! Then try back and forth, then clockwise circles, then counterclockwise. Watch it go! Is it a ghost?

No, it's you. Try as you might to keep your hand steady, your brain is transferring your imagined movement to your muscles, and they're responding with tiny contractions to start the motion. It doesn't feel like you're moving it, but you are.

Excellent. Well done! Now go and freak out your friends.

DEATH AND DYING

NOT QUITE GONE . . .

Rare as they are, real-life cases of people coming "back from the dead" (or rather, being mistaken for dead) can and do happen.

In 1977 a hearse crashed into a funeral home, the coffin flying out of the car and through a plate-glass window. Minutes later the "corpse" stepped out of the wreckage and into the street—the crash having roused him from a coma.

In 1994 an 86-year-old American woman spent over an hour in a body bag before a morgue worker noticed that the bag was breathing. And in 1996, two morgue workers in Havana, Cuba, were playing chess on the night shift when a body beside them sat up and moved the bishop three squares. In both cases, the "deceased" had suffered a heart attack and been mistakenly pronounced dead.

THE FEAR

Death and dying are the ultimate big, scary unknowns. Everybody eventually dies, but no one comes back to tell us what it was like. So in the absence of real knowledge, our fearful imaginations are left to run riot about how bad death and dying might be.

Can you "catch" death from dying people, like you catch a disease? Or does death come to "get" you, like a monster or a ghost? When it comes, do you fight it—struggling to stay in your body while someone (or something) tries to pull you away? Does it hurt? What if the doctors make a mistake and they bury or burn you alive? And once you are dead and buried, what's that like? Do you lie there in the grave feeling cold, hungry, or lonely? When will it happen? In 100 years? 50 years? Sooner?

THE REALITY

Death and dying are scary to most people because so much about them is uncertain or unknown. This raises a lot of questions that we have trouble answering, and not knowing the answers can make us even more afraid.

The truth is, we may never know for sure—while we're still alive—how death feels. But we do know quite a bit about what happens to our bodies during and after death. And that—at least—can answer some of these questions and make the whole thing seem a little less scary.

For starters, we know that death isn't a disease or a monster that comes to "get" you. It's a natural process that affects our bodies just as it affects flowers, trees, insects, and other forms of life. When we die, our bodies stop moving, and we stop eating, drinking, growing, and communicating with those around us. Then our bodies are recycled and absorbed back into the earth, air, and water of the environment. If our bodies are cremated (or burned), our scattered ashes feed and fertilize the earth. If our bodies are buried, then insects, worms, and bacteria* convert our bodies into nutrients, and these nutrients feed growing plants and animals for thousands of years after we die. So death forms part of a natural cycle that keeps all forms of life on Earth thriving and surviving.

Could we be buried alive by mistake? Well, no—not really. While this has certainly happened in the past, it's almost impossible nowadays. In the years before modern medicine, doctors or tribal healers would declare someone dead if they stopped breathing or their hearts stopped beating. But we now know that people can stop

---

* See? There go those bacteria being helpful again!

179

breathing (or even have their hearts stopped) for several minutes without dying—in some rare cases even longer. So doctors look for signs of brain activity instead of just breathing and heartbeat, using a machine that measures electrical signals in the brain, called an electroencephalogram (or EEG). If there is still activity in the brain, the doctors will keep working to bring you back to life. Only when all signs of life in the brain are gone (or when the breathing and heartbeat can't be restored after a long time trying) does the doctor pronounce someone dead.

We also know that being dead doesn't hurt, and you won't feel cold or hungry in the grave either. Pain, hunger, and sensitivity to temperature are all functions of a living body, designed to keep it alive, and they need living nerves to be transmitted and felt. So once your body has died, you can't feel pain, hunger, or cold anymore.

When we see death in movies, or read about it in stories, the dying person is often shown fighting for the last breath and struggling desperately to stay alive. But in reality, only a fraction of the thousands of people who meet death each day do it this dramatically. Most people aren't torn away

from their bodies, clinging to life. They die peacefully, already unconscious or asleep. Many people, of course, become very ill before they die. But most also have doctors, nurses, and caregivers to make sure they are comfortable and not suffering in their final days.

And while no one can predict exactly when this will happen to them, if you're young and healthy, chances are that it'll be a long, long time away.

THE CHANCES

Everybody dies of something, but for most people death is something that happens in old age and at the end of a long life. The most common causes of death are those linked to aging bodies, with organs and systems that gradually grow weak and fail. Among these, the heart and circulatory system (the name for the vessels and tubes the heart pumps your blood through) are the most likely things to finally give out.

In the developed world, for every 100 people who die, on average, around 57 will die peacefully in their sleep in old age— what's known as "natural causes." Another 20 will die of heart disease—when the heart stops pumping or blood vessels become brittle or clogged up. Another 14 will die of cancer, as cells within organs and tissues start to grow too fast and the body loses the ability to hold them in check. And another 4 or 5 people will die of a stroke, which is when a blood vessel leading to the brain becomes blocked, and part of the brain it supplies becomes damaged through lack of oxygen.

All of these conditions happen mostly to people well into old age. Now compare that with the remaining 4 in 100 who die sudden, early deaths from less natural causes (including everything from car accidents to fires, falls, drownings, shootings, and lightning strikes). Look at it that way, and you see that your odds of reaching a ripe old age—and of dying a peaceful death, rather than a sudden, violent one—are very good. And if you look after yourself and your body, you can make the odds even better.

THE LOWDOWN

Death is not an evil curse, a contagious disease, or a scary monster—it's a natural process that happens to our bodies just as it happens to the bodies of every plant, animal, mushroom, and microbe on the planet. Just as leaves change and fall to feed the earth, so do our bodies and those of every other living creature. The earth, in turn, feeds the plants, which feed the animals, which feed on each other, and eventually cycle their nourishing nutrients back to the earth once more. Without death, there could be no life—so in a way

we should be grateful for it.

If you've never experienced the death of someone close to you, death can seem scary because it's so mysterious and difficult to understand. Even if you have experienced this, it can still seem scary because it makes everybody feel so bad, and no one wants to talk about it.

When someone in your family (or even a much-loved pet) dies, it all seems so terrible because everyone is so sad. At funerals and burials, everyone is upset or crying. But this, too, is natural. We're sad that we won't get to be around them, to enjoy their company anymore. We're sad, then, for ourselves rather than for the person or pet who has died—after all, they can't feel sad or lonely anymore.

But once you've been through this, you eventually start to remember the person or pet as they were when they were alive, and you're happy and grateful for the time you got to share together. Although it can be very sad saying good-bye, you have the chance to understand death for what it is—neither good, nor bad, just a natural part of life itself.

Across the world, around 130,000 people die each day. But in the same day, 400,000 people are born. And so the cycle of life rolls on.

THE BEYOND

NEAR-DEATH EXPERIENCE

In 1970, Kimberly Clark Sharp was out walking when she had a sudden heart attack and dropped dead on the pavement. Doctors later revived her, but while she was (technically) dead, she had what is known as a Near-Death Experience (NDE). Here's how she described it:

"I knew I was not alone, but I still couldn't see clearly because I was enveloped in a dense, dark gray fog . . . Earthly time had no meaning for me any more. There was no concept of 'before' or 'after.' Everything—past, present, future—existed simultaneously. Suddenly, an enormous explosion erupted beneath me, an explosion of light rolling out to the furthest limits of my vision. I was in the center of the light. It blew away everything, including the fog. It reached the ends of the universe, which I could see, and doubled back on itself in endless layers. I was watching eternity unfold."

—From *After the Light* by Kimberly C. Sharp

THE FEAR For some people, dying isn't such a scary idea. They're convinced that a better world awaits them on the other side, and they have a pretty good idea of what it might look like. But others are far less certain, and for them "passing on" can be a terrifying thought because they're fearful of what might or might not lie beyond. After all, there's more than one idea about what could happen . . .

Do we sleep forever, never to wake again? Or do we come back to life (or reincarnate) into the body of another person or animal? If so, who or what will it be? A king? A president? A dolphin? A dung beetle? If another world awaits us beyond this one, then where is it and what will it look like? Will our friends and families be there too, or will we never see them again? And what will we be like? Will our "bodies" look the way they do during life? Or will they look older or younger? Will we have bodies at all? Will we recognize ourselves or others? Will we even remember who we were in our past lives? Think about it too much, and it can all get a bit overwhelming.

THE REALITY

Across the world, different peoples, cultures, and religions have very different ideas of what may lie beyond our mortal lives. For many Hindus and Buddhists, it's rebirth into another body and another life here on Earth. For most Christians, Jews, and Muslims, it's eternal life in another world far beyond and far different from ours—perhaps in another dimension or universe.

Japanese Shintoists walk a staircase to an afterworld with the spirits of their ancestors. Native American Indians pass on to the Happy Hunting Ground, where humans and animals live forever in eternal spring and summer. Some people believe there's nothing at all beyond this life—that we blink out like fireflies in the vast expanse of time and space. Others believe we burn more brightly than ever after death—our energy joining with that of everyone and everything that has ever lived, and expanding to fill the entire universe.

So who is right and who is wrong? What evidence do we have of what awaits us beyond death?

The truth is, we may never really know for sure because (at least for now) science isn't equipped to deal with questions about other dimensions and universes, or to explain the mystery of where our consciousness (or "thinking self") comes from, and where it might go after death.

Is there an afterworld in the sky above us? Well, no. We've journeyed into space and orbited the planet, and we can see there isn't. Could it be somewhere else in space—at the end of the universe, perhaps? Possibly. But as far we know, there is no space beyond the edge of our universe. According to cosmologists, the universe contains all the space there is, so it's either bordered by nothingness, or it wraps around on itself and so has no edge at all! But could there be another world in another dimension, or even another universe? Maybe so. Cosmologists say that there are almost certainly more dimensions and universes beyond ours. Do we go there after death? Who knows? It's possible.

What about being reborn, or reincarnated, into another body? Well, we have no evidence for that beyond a few stories about children (or even animals) who can recognize people from their "past lives," or people who say they can remember memories that aren't theirs. Could these stories be true? Possibly. Could the people involved be mistaken, or tricking themselves or others? That's possible too. No biologist has ever seen a person or animal reincarnate. But in a way, all of us are "reformed" into other bodies after death.

Our bodies decompose, and the atoms and molecules are recycled through soils, seas, microbes, plants, animals, and people. Your body definitely contains at least a billion atoms that were once fish, cows, trees, and lettuces. But since carbon atoms, especially, can circle the entire world in the seas and atmosphere, your body probably also contains at least a few carbon atoms that once belonged to Winston Churchill or King

Henry VIII. You might even contain an atom or two of dinosaur! And just as the material of our bodies is conserved and recycled throughout the planet, so too is the energy contained within it. And what happens to our thoughts and memories after we die? Do they just disappear, or do they go somewhere? And if so, do they migrate whole into new bodies, migrate into another dimension or universe, or just dissolve to join the energy of the known universe? Who can say?

THE LOWDOWN

The point is, whatever "the truth" about life after death may be, there's little sense being afraid of it just because we don't have all the answers. If you have strong religious beliefs then you may not be afraid, as you feel certain your idea of the afterlife is the right one. But even if you're not sure who's right and wrong, and you don't know what lies beyond, why be automatically afraid of it? If you're afraid of something, that means you know (or you're guessing) it will be bad. But whether it's another body, another life, another universe, or just a rejoining with the matter and energy of this one, nothing we know suggests that what happens to us beyond our lives will be bad or scary. So if you don't know for sure, why not guess that it'll be good instead? Hey—it works for me!

In the end, a fear of what you don't or can't know is just a fear of fear itself. It's phobo-phobia. And what's the point, or the fun, of that?

THE LAST WORD

o here we are at the end of our scary Fear Safari. We've seen almost every species of fear and phobia, and learned a lot of stuff along the way.

We found out that fear is both an emotion and a feeling. That emotions are physical changes that happen to the body. That feelings happen in the mind, partly in response to our emotions. And that by gaining a better understanding of our emotions, we can get better control of our feelings—including the feeling of fear.

We also discovered that some fears you're born with, and others you learn. The inborn fears evolved as part of a warning system, which helped our ancestors to survive in the past and still helps us to survive today. These include the fear of heights, darkness, drowning, snakes, and sudden movement.

I'M NOT SCARED!

As for the "learned" fears, they can develop in a number of different ways. We might learn them from experience, after a car crash or dog bite etches fear into our memories. More often, though, other people do the "etching" for us, as friends, family, books, magazines, TV, and movies can all create or exaggerate fears in our brains.

We found out why the feeling of fear builds and becomes worse with waiting, as anticipation leads to anxiety, dread, and panic. We found out that most fears come from a lack of knowledge—a kind of automatic suspicion against the unknown or as-yet unexplained. And perhaps most important of all, we discovered that exploring and explaining our fears are the first steps toward getting around them. Once fears become knowable and understandable, they're much easier to face. And if you want to face them, there are many ways to do it—both alone and with help from others.

It's been a crazy (and sometimes scary) ride, but I hope you felt it was worth it. If you now understand even a little bit more about the what, how, and why of your fears, then I think it was!

The world can be a big, scary place. But knowing yourself and knowing where your fear comes from can help you face it all with courage and curiosity.

As a wise man once said, why be a chicken when you can be a tiger?

Or, at the very least, an extremely brave chicken.

SOURCES

PHOTO CREDITS

INDEX